Everyday Conversations: The Key to the Contemporary Medium

Unlocking the Myths

Susan Fiandach

Connie Wake

**Everyday Conversations:
The Key to the Contemporary Medium**

Unlocking the Myths

Published by: **Bootstrap Publishing**

ISBN: 978-0692330630

First Edition, 2014
Printed in the United States of America

Dedication

We dedicate this book to all of the loved ones who have passed into the Other Side of Life, and have provided us with the experiences of this understanding.

Susan: I would like to thank my husband, Derek, and my children, Angelo, Dominic and Nina, for their continued belief in me. I love you all!

Connie: I would like to thank the family and friends who support me in my life, especially my children, Kevin and Kate, and stepson, Dean, for their love and support in this part of my life.

"You see, God always takes the simplest way."

--Albert Einstein

TABLE OF CONTENTS

Testimonials

"A clear, concise and positive overview of what mediumship today entails. Connie and Susan approach the topic of spirit communication from a practical and experiential point of view, acknowledging the underlying scientific principles that govern the Universe and explaining how those principles support and enhance the concepts of intuition, the ability to perceive those who are no longer in the physical world and the unified nature of creation. This book provides information valuable to those who seek only a basic framework to understand the phenomena of mediumship and will also be an excellent resource for experienced psychic mediums as an outline of how to conduct an ethical practice, including tips to keep one balanced and grounded."

Janet Dugan, Certified Spiritualist Medium, Licentiate Minister,
National Spiritualist Association of Churches

"Wow and at last!!! This masterpiece has the balance right, while intelligently written, the authors do not lose you throughout, with jargon, instead they have wonderfully explained universal concepts that most do not ever visit in a lifetime and have made them understandable. The authors speak to the layman, dabbler and professional in the same tone with the tremendous gift of never going over or under ones head.

A best seller in the making, *Everyday Conversations* is the finest book I have read on the subject in years. I wholeheartedly recommend this stunning piece of literature to whom ever has lost someone they loved and wanted to know whether communication with them was REALLY possible, so I guess anyone who has ever lived!"

Deborah Rees
International teaching medium, author and co-founder of Accolade Academy of Psychic and Mediumistic Studies
South Wales, UK

PREFACE

Hello and welcome! We'd like to say "we knew you were going to pick up this book" but in essence, *you* knew you were going to pick up this book...and that's why we wrote it.

Our purpose for writing *Everyday Conversations* is to offer our understanding of the definition and use of the sixth sense in our everyday lives. We do this in a way that dispels fears and myths to present a non-mystical and contemporary perspective of spirit communication. This is so that everyone has the opportunity to recognize and continue to be in touch with their loved ones even after they have passed into the next world we call The Other Side.

The service of the contemporary medium differs from that of generations ago. We live in the Information Age and so the expectation of the today's client would be to receive clear, relevant and helpful information. Today, there is no need for the darkened rooms, the heavy incense, a person in trance, and unfamiliar language to receive a psychic or medium reading. Our current understanding of science and spirituality has brought us to the point of re-defining the work and service of the psychic-medium.

And the character of today's psychic-medium is also being rewritten from that of the unknown and mysterious person behind the curtain to an everyday mom or dad raising a family. You will find the psychic-medium in a spiritual fair or expo, in a holistic salon or wellness center, or in the coffee shop down the street.

Our modern science confirms what the ancients knew—that our spirit is an unseen force and our connection to it is our intuition and expanded awareness. You can Google "psychic mediumship" and find a wealth of information on the subject, as well as local providers and teachers in your area. More and more people are checking it out and rightly so. Accessing our natural divination has gone beyond "the gift" and is becoming part of a spiritual experience, sought-after capability and service.

It just makes sense that now is the time to embrace a new awareness of psychic-medium communication and shed the mysticism and mythology. When we connect to those in Spirit, we are having a conversation. Just because the deceased loved one is no longer in a physical body and is in energy form doesn't change our ability to communicate with them. People do it more than they realize, but this form of communication is still shrouded in unknown and outdated beliefs. The ease and simplicity in which one speaks to another person at the coffee shop is the same ease and simplicity in which a conversation with someone in Spirit would flow.

The information in this book is a result of our learning, perspective, experience and... experience! We share our understanding of what it is to be psychic today, and how this sixth sense allows us to interact with both the physical and non-physical worlds. We not only hope to provide information, but also the sense that our divinity can be enjoyable. We have found that the Universe...God...has a sense of humor, and we have followed suit in how we view and use this connection.

We are each unique, however, and no two people will see, do and experience their world the same way. As with any learning opportunity, think about this perspective and take what works for you and your everyday life. At the very least, you have opened the door to another reality...explore, engage and enjoy the experience!

Explore

verb

: to look at (something) in a careful way to learn more about it : to study or analyze (something)

: to talk or think about (something) in a thoughtful and detailed way

: to learn about (something) by trying it

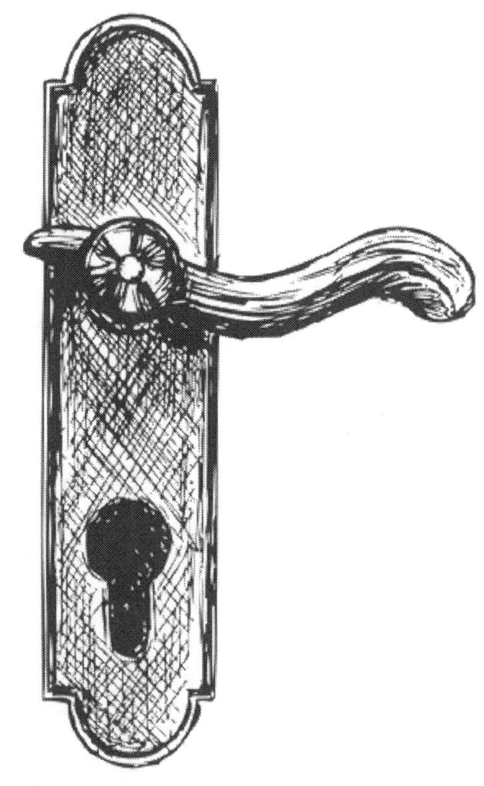

Chapter One

"Never say Never."

--Ella Kazan

"Picture it...Sicily"

Sophia Petrillo was a fictional character in the TV comedy show, *Golden Girls* and played the oldest of them all and "ma" to one of the other characters. When she would want to tell a story of her younger days, she would always start off by saying "picture it, Sicily, 19—"

So here is our "picture it." We'll talk about how it all started for us, and snapshots of stories of psychic medium experiences. Many of you have had interesting beginnings in your own psychic-ness. Personal experiences range from scary to cool, intermittent to nightly, understandable to bizarre. You may find similarities to the examples below, or hopefully, just plain interesting.

From these accounts, you will see that your experiences and feelings or sensations are not only fascinating but are valid and unique to your connection to the unseen world.

Susan was seeing and communicating with the deceased from a very young age. As the years passed her fear of what she experienced became stronger. As a Catholic raised in a second generation Italian American home, this was not considered "a good thing." Many years passed and in 2001 she was taken ill with a life threatening condition. As her body lie in a very fragile state in the hospital, her visits with those passed became clear again. Susan believed she had a near death experience, one that would change her life for the better. Susan has been working as professional medium since 2006 and says "my true state of being is back. Seeing, sensing, hearing and feeling those that have passed is who I am. Communicating with them as they are, present and accounted for!" Susan's tip: "Conversations with the dead are the same as conversations with the living...you just have to be a good listener."

While intuitive, Connie would have never considered herself a medium. There were the instances of hearing a voice in her head to "slow down" to warn of a car going through a red light at the upcoming intersection, or of a "you're welcome" when thanking God for arriving safely after driving through a horrendous rain storm. These and several incidents were before knowing what it was. It wasn't until her late 40's that she studied with a teacher to learn energy medicine, tarot, meditation as well as mediumship basics. Then the real fun began after learning how to understand and connect to her psychic-medium abilities *on purpose*. Connie's tip: Create that relationship with your self, your Self and the Universe and "Life is Good."

What's your story? Pretty much everyone, we believe, has had experiences of psychic-medium moments in their lives. We believe it is our natural channel to our Divine selves and that allows us a view into our connection to each other and the Universe.

Below are samples from our students, friends, clients and customers of the beginnings of their psychic adventure:

- Having a loved one die and thereafter feel like they are still around them from the scent of their cologne or perfume or smell of a cigarette.
- Having unexplained noises, footsteps, or things moving in the house.
- Having a child talk to or recognize the picture of a loved one passed whom they never met.
- Wanting to find out why they see repeating numbers or dreams.
- Having dreams of events that later come true.
- Seeing a shadow of a person or even an animal suddenly "out of nowhere" only to disappear in seconds.
- Seeing "something" in our peripheral vision and then having it vanish when turning to look at it.
- Feeling everyone around them and literally having to leave a large gathering of people.
- Having a psychic tell them "you are a healer" or "you are a medium."

- Having unexplained lights go out, the TV turn off or on.
- Seeing light sparks "in the air" for no apparent reason...and your eyes are fine!
- Having the thought of someone and then they call you or you run into them.
- Having unusual things, songs, events repeat over and over an inexplicable number of times, like finding pennies, feathers, hearing your deceased mother's name, etc.
- They believe or have been told there is an energy vortex in their home.

Here is an example of a story from someone who was not a practicing medium, or had any other awareness of spirit communication for that matter.

Sandra's husband, Charlie, got up very early each morning and was off to work by 6 am. Sandra, not being a morning person, would not get up so early to be with him. One morning as he was preparing to leave, Sandra woke up to a voice, very close and very loud, saying to her "tell him you love him...tell him now!" Sandra "just knew" that she needed to listen to this voice, and she shouted out "Hey Charlie, I love you and always will!" Charlie chuckled and replied "I love you too and I'll see you at 3" and went off to work. Before noon that day, Sandra received a call from the local hospital telling her she needed to come because her husband was there. Without the hospital saying it, she knew he had passed. While driving to the hospital, upset with the passing of her husband, a peace came over her as she remembered the exchange of their last words..."I love you."

We all have these stories. They are indications of what we know in our heart and soul to be true. Just as the discovery of the earth was not flat that launched humanity into the golden age of exploration, discovery that life is not just physical launches a golden age of enlightened awareness.

Skeptics

We believe that a degree of skepticism is healthy...it keeps us balanced. To have no skepticism at all is to be gullible. One has to weigh out all that we see, hear and read to make a judgment, especially in this age of spontaneous media that has no regard to validation and when dialogue is taken out of context in a news story.

For instance, there are many people watching TV shows on ghost investigations. Some of the participants are so desperate to see or hear something that any little squeak or shadow is considered paranormal. In many of these shows, the cast actually takes the time to disprove some claims or experiences. This is healthy, while also being a way to enhance the impact when something paranormal actually does happen.

When it comes to psychic-mediums, the skeptics can be daunting. They believe that all psychics are charlatans, fake and mimicking back what they see when a person sits in front of them, reading body language, eye and facial cues.

There are two types of skeptics.

1. The one who desires proof or evidence of the source of the information.
2. The one who resists being thought of as a "sucker" or being taken advantage of, and not willingly to participate fully.

The skeptic is looking for straight forward information—no generalizations. When a skeptic is the client, they are looking for information that would be undeniable: *"There is no way you would know that!"* kind of stuff. Skeptics will have that "a-ha" moment—not because they think you mentally put it there but that "a-ha" that you actually found that particular piece of evidence.

Here is an account of a reading given by Susan to Ron Z., a skeptic, from his point of view. While he was hoping to hear from his dad who passed two years earlier, he was skeptical about the process of mediumship *(is this stuff real?)* and was waiting for the piece of evidence.

> The night of the reading came and I reminded dad once again he better find Susan to come through! Sue took my hands and then in a very careful way told me that I seemed to be a person who judges people and that I should try to give

everyone the benefit of the doubt. I was ok with that because I know I am like that because of what I've done for a living for so long. Sue continued on to let me know that my dad was there described him to a "T". Being the skeptic that I was, I sat in that chair stone cold as could be and just let her keep talking. Yes, everything mentioned was him, but in my mind, a lot of the stuff could also be anyone. Except for one part! After Sue was done, she asked me if I had any questions. I asked to please go back to the part of the reading when she asked me if I had two siblings. At that time, I told her I had three siblings. Sue closed her eyes to ask the question again, and then opened them quickly saying "he just keeps saying 'three' with his three fingers in my face just like this" and Sue put her three fingers in my face. That's when I turned into a complete believer! I then explained that I am my dad's third son, and that years ago he started calling me "Three." If he called the house, it was "hey Three;" if I went over there, it was "hey Three" and so on. For the entire two weeks earlier, I had asked dad to come through with the "Hey Three!" and he did. I was stunned...it was simply awesome!

This is an example of an "a-ha" moment of a skeptic...he now believes in life continues after death and that we can always have a conversation with our loved ones.

The Spiritualist Movement and the Fox Sisters:

In the mid 1800's, there were two young girls in Upstate NY who began communicating through a series of raps and taps with a spirit they later described as a murdered carpetbagger. They became famous for their spirit communications and performed demonstrations of their abilities. This is what prompted

Spiritualism to become a religion so people would benefit from the liberty and safety of religious freedom for their beliefs of life beyond death.

However, this also prompted fear and disbelief and people set out to disprove their work. Eventually, the stresses of this notoriety and physical abuse they suffered to prove their work was overwhelming and caused them to recant their original abilities and experiences. People began to have séances in their homes for "entertainment purposes" eventually getting to well-attended, staged events. This prompted accusations of fraudulent behavior.

Not all mediums are members of the Spiritualist religion but the Spiritualist movement allowed mediums to become more main stream without fear. The history of this has followed mediumship and the resulting skepticism needs to be addressed by the professional medium often.

From the skeptic to a believer, there are all kinds of incidents that cannot be explained. Whatever your story is, whether a "weird "experience," that little voice intuitive moment or coincidence just won't explain it, we invite you to take it further to transform the unknown, the known. You may find that *your* universe gets bigger!

CHAPTER TWO

"For whoever exalts himself will be humbled, and whoever humbles himself will be exalted." –Bible, Matthew 23:12

It's not our gift...

Remember that Seinfield episode about the label-maker "re-gift" and the hubbub about regifting? Well, the psychic-medium is the ultimate re-gifter...and you may hear a lot of hubbub about this as well!

Who has the gift? The gift comes from Spirit or those who have passed in the form of communication and the psychic-medium relays that information to the client. The medium is given that gift, and then re-gifts it to the client...the medium does not own the gift.

To believe that one is "gifted" is to consider being above one who doesn't have the gift, to separate from normal folk, and to make oneself special. When that belief is in place, the information received and delivered becomes skewed through the filters of the medium. Filters are our personal beliefs and the core understanding of our awareness of who we are, and the expression of those beliefs and understanding through our thoughts, words, habits and actions.

If the psychic medium is holding onto a belief that "I have a gift" it can foster separateness and self-centeredness, and the unbalanced ego comes into play, affecting the essence of the information from Spirit. The other thing that may get negatively influenced is the client's free will and choice due to their state of mind. A client's free will and choice should never be compromised as a result of a reading.

An ego is not a bad thing...it is part of our humanity and we flex it often as we go through our day. If you have a healthy ego, you generally have a good understanding of self, have self-worth, and have a sincere respect for the work being done and the client being served. You are confident and able to set aside personal opinions and judgments to be an impartial observer, an unbiased reporter and a clear interpreter in your work.

An unhealthy ego has two sides that can influence a medium's reading. A self-centered or bloated ego will superimpose this self-importance onto the reading. All of a sudden, "I have a gift" becomes "and you don't so you should listen to what I have to say" reading. A client who comes in confused or overwhelmed takes advice given with this dominance as gospel and their decision-making is negatively influenced.

In this age of "knowledge is power," people have absorbed all sorts of information through their studies and experiences, not only through higher education but through the internet, magazines, and impressive and well-stocked book stores. People do have a lot to say about a variety of subjects, so it makes sense the ego takes over to proclaim their position. The information the medium is giving from Spirit should be relayed as given, and not be prejudiced by the opinion of the medium. The medium's ego has no place in the reading.

The other aspect is the *need* to say "I have a gift" as a self-validating affirmation that has underpinnings of fear and self-doubt on the part of the medium. While some may say "this is a God-given gift" we are here to tell you that everyone has this God-given gift as a natural aspect of our being. People don't go around telling others of their God-given gift of seeing or hearing, so why would the sixth sense be any different? Consciously or sub-consciously, "I have a gift" also says "look what I can do" which gets woven into the words, phrases and messages of the reading that may captivate the client instead of serve the client. Again, the client's free will is influenced not by the empowerment of Spirit messages but by the attention-seeking medium.

Communication from Spirit is from the realm of unconditional love and upliftment, providing messages of hope, comfort and validation. The path of the medium is to know where they are from an ego perspective so that the guidance and messages received are as true and sincere as possible. This self-reflection process is what we refer to as the art of mastering the self, and is discussed further in Chapter 5.

Chapter Three

"If we all did the things we are capable of doing, we would literally astound ourselves.

–Thomas A. Edison

Our Natural Channel

In order to talk about Spirit and the ability to converse with those who have passed, we also need to include the universe that this ability resides in. Our current understanding of the Universe stems from collected views from readings, the accounts of Sue's near-death experience, and the current understanding of the physics of the Universe.

We start with the universe as a field of pure energy. This quantum theory of a Unified Field creates a oneness of the energy of everything. To that, we add God Consciousness. We refer to this approach as:

Define Your Universe
Divine Your Universe

Our understanding of the universe aligns with the theory that everything is energy. The Big Bang unleashed this energy to create the universe, from the sub-atomic quantum scale to the classical scale of the physical universe, such as the galaxies, planets, the sun, earth including physical life on earth. These energies are governed by laws of energy and matter, verifiable by mathematical formulas, interacting the same way to always do what they will always do. Judgment does not affect these energy/matter laws. For example, the law of gravity always does the same thing...if a good person and a bad person were to fall off a cliff, both would hit the ground.

To define your universe is to settle on what it is and how it works for you. If you believe the universe is subjective and depends on the circumstance or the case at hand, you will need a set of ground rules to keep track of the various scenarios. In other words, if you have a fear-based understanding of life, you will believe and act to maintain the fears. You will look for protection, rationalization of why "bad things happen to good people," validation of what you believe, justification for the ill acts of others, etc.

In our definition of the universe, we follow a “keep it simple” philosophy, also referred to as Ockham's Razor. This is a principle attributed to a 14th century Franciscan friar, William of Ockham, which basically states when you have two competing theories that can produce the same outcome the simpler one is the better.

So now we look to “divine our universe.” God Consciousness at its purest level is “Unconditional Love, Infinite Wisdom and Unlimited Power of Creation” (from the teachings of White Eagle Lodge). Birthed from the purest form of God Consciousness (made in Its image) is the High Self. We exist at this level with full consciousness as a divine being, with total knowledge of our purpose and motives, in the full grace of God.

As this High Self, there isn't anything we don't know, can't get to, or can't have in our universe. The High Self sets out to adventure in the duality of the universe governed by a set of unwavering universal laws, such as the Law of Attraction, the Law of Cause and Effect, the Law of Polarity, etc. (You can Google the 7 Hermetic Laws for more details here.)

In this adventure and to capture all of the experiences is the Soul aspect of our High Self. The soul acts as a depository of all of our lives, including our current one, holding the memory of all life experiences, the wisdom gained, lessons learned, and karmic balances. These memories are accessible not only by us but also by the medium.

At the next experience of consciousness is our physical being, and completes the channel from our self, to our Soul, to the High Self and God Consciousness...and back. This channel is used for divination, communication, healing (as in the energy healing arts and our own guidance). At our physical level, the energy centers along our nervous system (called chakras), our physical senses and our sixth sense interpret the physical and non-physical energies around us.

When we talk of Spirit, we are considering the energy of consciousness, meaning the force that connects the pure potential energy of the Unified Field and the pure Consciousness of the Divine. As Spirit, energy and consciousness are unhindered by emotional suffering, judgments and restrictive dogma. We keep our definition and divination of our universe as the pure potential and unconditional love that it is, redefining the process of psychic-mediumship, instead of the other way around. In other words, to explain how we interact with the non-physical world, we consider the pragmatic nature of energy and consciousness. Can you give a reading to someone 3,000 miles away, or who has "just passed?" Yes, because energy and consciousness are instantly connected...there is no time or space boundaries. So instead of changing the universe to fit the belief, we change the belief.

These are key elements on how one goes forward in psychic-medium studies. *Defining* your universe is your understanding what makes the universe tick and your role in it. *Divining* your universe is your understanding of God Consciousness, and who you are in that. Whatever your beliefs are will create the way you interpret the world. For example, if you believe in God who punishes people for being bad, your reading for someone who committed suicide will be influenced. By working with the instinct of your physical being (the universe) and the intuition of your non-physical being (consciousness) will make available an infinite view of the playing field, or a narrow one.

We are now understanding what Pierre Teilhard de Chardin, French philosopher and Jesuit priest of the early 1900's meant by: "We are not human beings having a spiritual experience. We are spiritual beings having a human experience." Our reality starts with an understanding of who we are and the kind of universe we are in...we create it all.

The Universe and the Medium

If our physical selves are a version of energy, and those who have passed are also a version of energy, we then should be able to connect energy to energy, consciousness to consciousness, and communicate. We have a natural channel between our High Self and our physical being to receive, send and understand energy in the form of thoughts as interpreted by the brain from all the senses, including intuition.

When we physically sense something, the cells transport the signal to the brain and the brain tells us what it is...through sight, sound, touch, smell or taste. Here's the kicker...this does not only apply to the physical world. We don't normally think that our physical senses pick up information from the non-physical world, but consider the following:

You see a rose. Your senses tell you it is deep red in color, has velvety petals, and a distinctive fragrance. This is matter and the interpretation of information through the physical senses.

You sense a rose. There is no rose present. You smell its distinctive fragrance, the memory of its soft petals is impressed upon you and you know it's a beautiful deep red. This sudden sense of the rose reminds you of your grandmother and you feel she is right there. This is an interpretation of non-physical information through the brain's processing of a physical sense. This is sensing and interpreting Spirit.

It's all one sense...the brain doesn't know if it's a physical or non-physical sense.

You've heard of the term, gut instinct or gut feeling. This is an interpretation of your body sensing the energy around a person, place or thing and communicating that back to your brain.

We all have instinct and intuition.

Our instincts are part of the brain that runs automatically. Instincts are survival and evolution based...flight or fight. You may think of those instincts that are so automatic from our experiences that they happen spontaneously. These types of instincts may be tied into your experiences with people, for example, when you come across an angry person, you may not engage them...you know better! Your experiences gave you the instinctive insight to "walk away."

Intuition would be feeling the anger from that person before you see it or they exhibit it to you. The names or experiences of intuition that we've all heard are:

> Gut feeling
>
> I have a hunch
>
> I just knew
>
> I had a feeling ...
>
> I heard a small voice... in some religions, it's the angel or the devil but it's us.

> When you think about someone and suddenly they call you or you run into them.
> Or you dream about something and the event occurs.

Deja vu is a form of intuition. It is when you feel as though you've already had the experience, been somewhere, or had a conversation with someone. This can be considered psychic processes in the non-physical realm that has no time. We can get impressions or thoughts ahead of time or we may remember impressions or thoughts of previous incarnations from the Soul.

Intuition sometimes counters critical thinking...because we over think and start bringing into our reality our fears, hopes, biases and judgments.

When we are born, our brain runs our body, all the natural functions we need. The life experiences, either enhances or dilutes our intuitive side. You may hear that children are naturally intuitive until they get to 5 or 6 years old, then the regimen of life takes over from parental beliefs, cultural, society, religions, etc.

We need to re-ignite the senses, including the intuitive sense, and integrate it with an understanding of an energy universe and the consciousness of Oneness. Energy is energy, governed by Universal (or Natural) Law. Interpreting the energy is a part of being intuitive, a.k.a., psychic, and the channel to this information is who we are as divine beings to Source.

Chapter Four

"When we become a part of anything, it becomes a part of us."
–David Harold Fink

"It's Energy, People!"

If everything is energy, everybody is feeling it!

If we were to look at a day in the life of various people, we might see how energy affects them in their work and play...even if they don't know it.

<u>Hairdresser or in the Beauty/Spa industry</u>: This is one of the only professions other than medical that people allow you to touch their physical body; in fact they invite you to do so. Like bartenders, many hairdressers feel that people sit in the chair and open up and tell us their life story, their private thoughts, and what is going on in their world. Susan has been a hairdresser for 36 years and has come to understand this from an energy viewpoint.

"I believe that when the hairdresser touches the head and shoulders of the client, they immediately open up their energy to us. In essence, invite us in." Where the hairdresser stands is a key point here. They are standing with their heart open to the back of the client's head. The client's head and neck are the focal point of Spiritual energy, following the chakra centers of the throat, forehead (or third eye) and crown (top of the head).

Chakra is Sanskrit for wheel and pertains to the energy areas of the body. The heart chakra is also referred to as the "seat of the soul" and is immensely affecting the connection person to person. The hair dresser is immersed in the client's aura/energy and engages the client through their energy centers at the throat, third eye and crown. There is communication without words, intuitive exchanges and non-physical cues. The hair dresser will become used to a regular clients' energy and so the non-verbal communications become stronger. This is true for anyone working in the salon/spa industry because of their constant physical connection to the person.

<u>Medical Profession – Nurses, Therapists, Trainers, etc.</u> In the medical profession, most often, patients are in a vulnerable state, being in matters of life and death. When one is unwell, you have to trust the medical personnel, and trust is key. Letting your guard down, trusting, and being open with people near you, the channel for communication, both physical and non-physical, is activated. Again, the energy centers come into play and all seven major chakras are affected and open.

Nurses are particularly open to receiving the non-physical connection. Most are empathic, able to feel another's emotional state, and understand the power of touch and energy therapy, whether they are formally trained or not.

<u>Police</u> are usually intuitive, going with the gut feelings or hunches. Their training and in fact their survival, depends on

understanding the non-verbal information in people, places and things.

Moms and Dads – this is a duh

Animal Lovers, Vets and Staff – The ultimate non-verbal communication. There are a lot of testimonials of telepathy between humans and animals. If you have a pet of your own, you come to understand what they need. You understand them and they understand you...without a spoken word.

Tellers, Cashiers, Wait Staff – The exchange of energy through money. Sensing energies and getting information through objects by touch is called psychometry and it can happen spontaneously or on purpose.

Daycare Providers – Being a pseudo parent, and the need to connect with those who cannot yet speak.

Teachers – How to interpret each person's thoughts as they strive to teach their material.

Artists – This is the classic definition of the right brain where imagination and intuitive information closely lie. The imagination is what let's us see the information we are intuitively picking up.

Landscapers/Gardeners/Farmers – The natural connection to Earth and Mother Nature is an innate way to receive information from our environment and living things. The person with a "green thumb" naturally understands and works with the subtle energies from the Earth and plant life.

Clergy, Funeral Directors/Staff – They are connected by their belief system and faith, and the service to comfort those in need. Through empathy, intuitive expressions are received. They naturally know what to do in their work.

In summary, everyone has a connection to the energy around us, and the communication – the passing of information from the physical to the non-physical – is always available. Being mindful to the matter and energy around us and interacting with it purposefully is what is referred to as being "awake and aware" on our path to enlightenment.

Chapter Five

"Know thyself."

–Socrates

Me, Myself and I

You may be saying to yourself "hmm...what is all this psychic stuff and why should I believe it's a real thing"? If that's the case we would like you to think about why you feel you need to qualify (make real) intuition? Why do we as intelligent people push away a concept that does not include proof by current physical science methodology? Why do we not believe what we feel we cannot see? Why then, is religion so prevalent? Wars rage over religious beliefs. Isn't this a belief in that which is not seen? Isn't that what faith is? To believe in what we cannot see?

Let's explore this further.

See what you feel
Feel what you hear
Hear what you sense
Sense what you know
Know what you believe
Believe in yourself

--Susan Fiandach, 2010

The fact of the matter is to be human is to be intuitive, and to be intuitive is to be psychic. This is our natural, born selves. As we grow older, we forget about these innate understandings of the total being we really are. Our intellect tells us ignore the intangible information and we go back to five-sensory living, existing just on a physical level. We no longer trust our natural sixth sense, our intuition, our psychic sense. Most people toss around the term "psychic" while bristling at the association, when in fact it is a real aspect of life.

Our brains have much more to offer than just five physical senses...to work in a way that allows us to see what isn't there to see, to hear what isn't said, and to feel without a touch.

Quoting Andrew B. Newberg, M.D. in the 2004 movie, *What the Bleep Do We Know?*

> *Our brain receives 400 billion bits/second of information, but we're only aware of 2000 bits/second. Reality is happening in our brain all the time — we're receiving it but it's not being integrated.*

We understand this to mean the potential of receiving and interpreting information at all levels, physical and non-physical, is in our grasp. While we are not saying we would need to know everything the mind is collecting from its environment (both outside of the body and inside the body), we are saying there is more information already in play. Relearning and trusting what is naturally ours to receive is to accept our true self.

Understanding the self is an important element in understanding mediumship, not only in terms of accessing mediumship, but also in terms of the quality of mediumship as a service.

The true self is sometimes referred to as the soul, but we are talking about the true self that integrates all the aspects of the self—physical, emotional, mental—as well as the spiritual. The everyday self or physical self is concerned with survival, comfort and security. The emotional self is concerned with recognition, acceptance, relationships, and belonging. The mental self is concerned with understanding what life is, validating and interpreting the world around us, relief and balance. And, of course, the spiritual aspects look at life on a greater scale and our connection to our Universe.

Outside influences such as environment, childhood, religious or cultural customs may dictate how we behave, what we believe and what we think our reality is. We can understand our physical reality, our emotional balance, and our mental abilities through the input and interpretation of our five physical senses. We tend to ignore, doubt or override the influence and impact of a spiritual connection, the part that our sixth sense is accessing. To bring these aspects together, to integrate mind, body and spirit, we need to open our consciousness to the physical and non-physical domains of our reality, and this is done through awareness and expression of all six senses.

Our consciousness is self awareness, its connection to others, and its connection to the greater Consciousness of the universe. When we go about our day-to-day in almost a robotic or unaware state, we don't engage our consciousness to its full extent. We focus our minds only on the physical cues of our body ("I'm hungry") or the environment (it's cold outside"). Our emotions are reactions to the latest news, the argument with our loved one, the people at work, etc. And our mental abilities are taxed with stress and burdens of survival instead of inspiration and creativity. If we find ourselves in this state, it is also referred to "suffering" or trapped by the ego, which has a very narrow view of how to live life. We have an ego, which cannot be ignored because it is there for our survival in a physical world, but it can be managed so that the authentic self is the master of the ship.

To engage this authentic self that awakens our consciousness to all life that is happening around us is typically referred to as our life path. It is our attempt to balance the physical, emotional, mental and spiritual aspects of our self. This expanding awareness and mindfulness of expression is the journey of becoming our best selves. This journey has to start with the belief and understanding of all you see, sense, hear, and feel the expanded view and relationship with the physical and non-physical worlds...Earth and Heaven. You are a divine self and believing in your self matters.

But just like an airline attendant would say *"If you are traveling with a child or someone who requires assistance, secure your mask on first, and then assist the other person"* to be of service to others, there is a duty to the self. Knowing who we are is one of the key values of those who regularly touch in with their intuitive, psychic nature to serve others. The awareness of self provides the framework for the expression of beliefs that influences our service to another, in a way that is positive, empowering and sincere.

To understand this relationship of expression and self awareness, see figure 1.

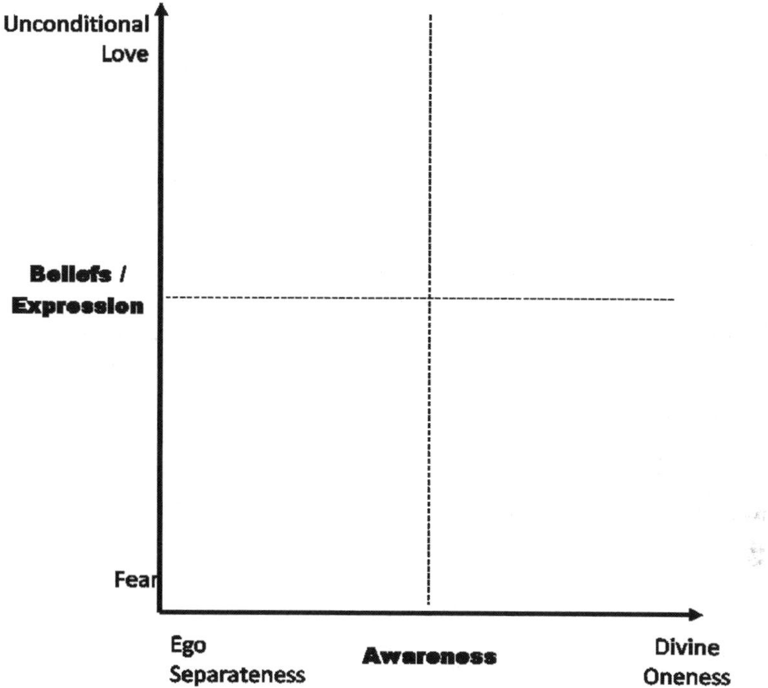

A way to look at where we are along our spiritual journey—a journey of self discovery—we can think of it as what we believe and how we express it and the awareness of who we are in the universe of it all.

At one end of the vertical axis is the Divine quality of Unconditional Love and at the other end is the physical self of fear. The horizontal axis shows the Divine quality of Oneness at one end and the physical self of ego (or separateness) at the other.

Our beliefs, as expressed by our attitudes and emotions, vary along the vertical axis...from fear, lack, jealousy, doubtfulness, worry, prejudice, pessimism, etc., to collaboration, cooperation, confidence, joy, gratitude, friendship, optimistic, etc. Our daily life is a reflection of our beliefs, expressed by our thoughts, words and actions.

Our awareness of our self will vary from self-ish to self-less, from considering just our survival and comforts to considering the survival and comforts of all. We can live in fear and the self-importance of the ego or in the full awareness of our own divinity in expressions of love, compassion and joy...and, anywhere in between.

The purpose of this diagram is to be aware of our self-talk and the expression of our beliefs in relation to our connection to each other and the Divine. The conversation between Spirit and the medium, and between the medium and the client, needs to be as loving and compassionate as possible, clear from our own internal struggles of fear, doubt and ego. We are not saying a professional medium has mastered her/himself as Jesus or the Buddha. We are saying that this awareness of self and expression to others, through all the senses and understanding, enables one to be as clear a channel to Spirit as possible. To provide messages of love, comfort, evidence and empowerment is the quality measure of the professional psychic-medium today.

Chapter Six

"We are what we think. All that we are arises with our thoughts. With our thoughts, we make our world."

–Gautama Buddha

The Here After ... or After Here

A psychic-medium reading is an interaction between "the two worlds" of the non-physical and physical. Even though we refer to "the other side" as a place, these worlds are side by side. Or you can think of it as the hereafter...meaning they are "here" when "after" they leave the physical.

Mary lived in her home with her mother for more than 30 years. For Mary to have her mom in the home was the norm. When her mom passed, she did so quietly in her sleep, and Mary found her body the next morning. Ever since that day, both Mary and her husband would hear sounds of her mother stirring in her own room, and even saw the mother walking down the hall to the bathroom. When asked if Mary and her husband were afraid, they replied "No, mom loved us and would never harm us." Although no longer in her physical form, the energy of Mary's mother was going about her daily business as she always did.

There are a variety of understandings regarding the Other Side, what it is and how to communicate with loved ones there. And, there are many self-imposed rules that most mediums may follow to do that.

For example, a psychic-medium may believe they are not able to communicate because:

- The loved one has just passed and cannot be contacted yet
- The loved one is "in classes" or "taking care of business" and is not available.
- They have already reincarnated and are not available.
- The loved one is "earth bound" and cannot be contacted. This is used a lot for people who have committed suicide or passed from a traumatic death.
- The loved one did not speak the same language as the medium

Let's address these things. The moment you pass, you are in the non-physical. Communication can happen immediately because thought is energy and is not impeded by time, distance or circumstance. The soul inherits the memories of the experiences and life lived. The "spirit" of the loved one and the High Self are the same...back in the field of pure potential, unconditional love and free will. Actually the physical self and the High Self are always integrated...so consider the unlimited nature of a spirit and Spirit, the High Self and Source, whether considered live or dead. Energy is energy, consciousness is consciousness...there are no barriers, heavens or hells, here or there.

There are people, including mediums, who have had contact with those who have passed from the moment they do so. Hospice workers will often report seeing mist or fog come off the physical body at the moment of passing, or see the person standing in the hallway of a hospital or nursing home.

Children will often have first hand, direct communication with loved ones. Susan's three year old nephew was in a sound sleep in his own home when suddenly he woke up, lifted his head, waved saying "bye-bye grandma, I'll miss you" at the exact time of Susan's mother's passing at the hospital.

Why then would a medium not be able to connect within hours or weeks? It is possible but because some mediums have this self-imposed rule of a barrier between them and the spirit, they create their inability to communicate...thoughts are things. The spirit of the person has changed and exists differently than in a physical state, but it's not a separate place.

Connie: I got the call from the nursing home that my mom had passed. After a long evening of taking care of the necessary arrangements, I returned home exhausted. Before I fell asleep, I asked Spirit to give me a sign that my mom was with the loved ones who had passed before her. At that moment in my mind's eye, I saw two images. One of my mom as a young woman running to her mother; and another image immediately following of that of my mom as a young bride, hugging my dad as a young soldier in his WWII uniform. Within hours of passing, I received strong evidence from my mom.

The learning is here...not on the Other Side. The High Self is already divinely perfect as a direct spark of God. The soul is the depository of all life experiences and keeps the wisdom of those experiences to carry through to the next "mission". There is no more learning to be done "there"...it is here. So the spirit of the loved one as the High Self is ready and able to communicate because they are not in school or anywhere else. They are "here after."

Reincarnation is not an all-or-nothing deal. We are not here OR there. The memories of experiences, of existences, of lives, are in the soul as energy and accessible through the medium. The medium is communicating with the energy of the person that lived.

The energy is the memory of their life's experiences, so the medium accesses the memory of the life lived and interprets it back as the reading.

In regards to earth-bound spirits, if we are dealing with the energy of memory, how would it get stuck anywhere? The memory will always be with us, in the energy of the living, and can be accessed. Again, there is no "here" or "there" and because all conscious beings have free will and choice, no one is "stuck" anywhere they don't want to be. In the case of ghosts, this may be very strong residual energy or the person who wants to be a ghost and show themselves.

As it relates to suicides or traumatic deaths, there is a belief that suicides are in a purgatory or not where everybody else is. Or a very traumatic death causes the energy to "stay" on Earth. Again, free will and choice, but most importantly, in a universe of unconditional love, this wouldn't happen. There is no judgment to assign a spirit to any particular place, let alone not to have them accessible.

In our experiences, all those who have committed suicide have shown themselves with other loved ones who have also passed. Along with those who have had a traumatic passing, they communicate a sense of peace, happiness and completeness. The medium is accessing the energy of the memory and brings information regarding the life and death of the individual, therefore accesses their closure of life's process. The loved one who passed is not reliving the experience and there would be no block to the information.

In the case of someone committing a horrific crime or murder, the information is the information. They are not in judgment, their spirit is intact, and there is no spiritual defect. These crimes were committed here, in life, in the imperfect human condition, made even more imperfect by mental and emotional illness.

So in the case of an ego affecting a reading, the medium would bring into play the judgment of the person and his/her crime, and possibly speak of karma, restitution, hell, etc.

In the case of a language barrier, a medium can still pick up the essence of the person who has passed, regardless of language, age, cultural, or physical limitations. Most people have heard of the term, telepathy, which is a means a communication without the known (physical) senses. Non-physical sense has no language or cultural barrier, for example, infants and animals.

If I'm not going anywhere then what am I doing?

Conventional beliefs would say there are planes of existence to be crossed to go from the physical to the non-physical realms. In the case of mediumship, it is said the mediums must go to the astral plane to receive the thoughts from those who have passed. The one who has passed must "descend" to that plane in order to interact with the physical plane.

Most mediums also feel they need to go "up" to the astral plane, because it is felt that Spirits vibrate at a higher frequency than us. Most mediums refer to this as "raising their vibration."

Is "raising your vibration" to get happy? Do you need to be full of energy? Is it a state of mind? Yes, but not a plane of mind! Most often, when a person has an experience that they feel is Spirit oriented, they are fully engaged in a mundane activity. Their brain activity has lowered, the thinking brain quiets and thus opens our other senses. The brain activity is measured in hertz (HZ) and when a person is sleeping, meditating or deeply involved in thoughtless activity, this can be measured. Why then, would we need to raise our vibration when ultimately, it would serve us best to slow our brain down.

However, we find this confusing from our point of view in everyday conversation. We challenge this as it is not necessary in "everyday conversations" with each other, so why would the Universe be different?

There are times you are just going through your day and suddenly you smell your deceased mom's perfume. And you know it was a visit from your mom. So how did that happen?

Did you "do something" to get that scent? Or did your mom "do something" to send it? Did either one of you go to the astral plane?

We believe, no. This is everyday conversation between the physical and non-physical worlds. You do not need to know about the planes of existence, the spirit does not need to "be ready" to connect with you, etc. She intended it...you received it. It's really no more than a thought. Thought is universe, physical and non-physical! Thoughts become things, whether we are manifesting stuff or the exchange of ideas into messages.

This is the Webster definition of communication..."the act or process of using words, sounds, signs, or behaviors to express or exchange information or to express your ideas, thoughts, feelings, etc., to someone else." Alive or dead.

Whether it's a thought from a soul (mediumistic), or a thought from a living being (psychic), thought is energy and we all send, receive, interpret through our senses. This is how communication takes place with those who passed or an energy exchange between each other from right here right now.

Chapter Seven

"Order and simplification are the first steps toward the mastery of a subject..."

--Thomas Mann

#SpiritGuides

In home towns or on the Hollywood stage, "What is my Spirit Guide's Name?" is a common question to psychic-mediums. You may have heard people talk about spirit guides or their guides, teachers or animal totems and you think "what the heck are they talking about?"

Spirit Guides is the general term that applies to our team in the Spirit (or energy) realm and can include loved ones and what most people know as our Guardian Angel. They assist us on that grand adventure we set off to do here.

There are many schools of thought in regards to Spirit Guides...what they do, how many we have, etc. There is a traditional school of thought on the roles and responsibilities of a network of non-physical beings available to us as guides on our earthly journey. When you go on the internet, this may be the only explanation of spirit guides you see.

In the traditional view, we have this network at our disposal right from birth, well actually, before birth. We plan this physical existence and the reason(s) for incarnating, and the planning committee is our High Self and those who act as our guides and teachers in this life. From this "pre-life" planning, we know what we want to do and have people both in physical and non-physical form to help us do it.

Creating a working relationship starts with knowing who they are. Here are examples of "spirit guide jobs" most commonly referenced:

Master Guide – This is a the "big Kahuna" guide who we planned our Earth tour with and is in charge of the rest of our Guide team, holding us to the master plan and available for guidance at this high level.

Doctor Guide – This guide assists in healing work for ourselves and others and on all levels – physical, mental, emotional and spiritual. This guide can also show up if you work in the medical field, energy wellness therapies, etc.

Native Guide – This guide is said to be of the native land you are connected to, and brings to you ancestor energies and wisdom.

Protector Guide – This guide can work with us on a physical and spiritual level, in our daily lives as well as our spiritual work. A protector guide is the one who is the bouncer at our spiritual door to keep out the riff-raff of the Universe so we can go confidently forward with our work with minimal disruptions or issues.

Joy Guide – This is the "don't sweat the small stuff" guide that reminds us to laugh and play. Joy guides are also said to be impish at times when we need to not take ourselves so seriously, by hiding our keys or moving an object that we know we just put down. Joy guides make us pause...breathe...and then keep going.

Helper Guide – The helper guide or sometimes called teacher guide is a general name to any and all of the guides that step in to work with us during specific times of our lives. We can ask for these guides to help us in school, in a relationship, complete an art or work project, etc.

Animal or Nature Spirit Guide – This is a connection to our Earth through Mother Nature through her animal and elemental (fairies, gnomes, etc). We can connect with the characteristics of these beings and also listen to their guidance and receive their support.

We can connect with our Spirit Guides through intention and commitment. However, the Spirit Guides are always in service to the High Self, the one who has the master plan and doing the work. Spirit Guides (as well as Angels and Ascended Masters) will never interfere in the free will and choice of the individual. Some of the ways our Spirit and our Spirit Guides connect with us is through inspired thought, sometimes referred to as our intuitive voice, as well as gut feelings, "voices in our heads", dreams, etc. We can initiate (and respond) contact by opening a channel, through meditation, journaling, and purposeful intent to be mindful and consciously aware of who we are and what we are doing and being. Spirit Guides can be very active or very quiet...they can be asked for every situation or just the important ones. However, because we have free will and choice, Spirit

Guides, Teachers and Angels are to assist only, and not take precedence over our thoughts, decisions and actions of our journey.

But there is another side to the understanding of Spirit Guides and the High Self. This is our point of view and completely different from the traditional thoughts and beliefs expressed above.

What brought us to this position are two main concerns: (1) Why would we have to have other beings attached to us for teaching and communicating purposes; and (2) why would we be able to work with them, and only them, for life direction and assistance?

One of the most common things we fear is having an attachment to our self or soul by a discarnate entity. Hollywood and TV play this up very well, and ignorance perpetuates it when anything we don't understand pops up in our awareness. In the traditional view of spirit guides, it is usually suggested to "find the highest and best" guides to work with you and be leery of "low vibration guides." You see here the mixed message in regards to the need and attachment of entities to us, for whatever reason. The laws of the universe are non-judgmental. As in the law of gravity, the good and the bad fall off the cliff and hit the ground below. Likewise, there would not be a set of rules for positive attachments and another set for negative attachments. Attachments either are...or are not. More on this in the next chapter.

The other concern raises the question of why a separate group of beings would be needed to access guidance and life direction from the High Self. We have a direct connection to our High Self and the wisdom of the Infinite Mind of the universe. And, as stated earlier, we also believe the soul is a depository of accumulated experiences and wisdom of all of our incarnations (a.k.a. past lives) as well as our current life. We have at our disposal our own "soul library" of understanding and information on various aspects of life, and therefore, a clear and direct communication channel to it. We can access this directly.

We have been the priest, the slave, the artisan, the warrior! We already have what it takes to be the captain of the ship in this Earth adventure. The interpretation of vibrations we feel as Spirit Guides may be various aspects of our High Self from wisdom collected through all of our lives. In other words, The Spirit Guide is You!

If we look at the traditional role of Spirit Guides, such as the Master Guide/Teacher, Protector, Native Guide, Doctor Guide and Joy Guides, what aspects of our self and High Self would we access to cover the attributes needed or the jobs to be done to assist us in the here and now?

Let's go through the most common and compare the two views:

<u>Master-Teacher Guide</u> is a vibration we sense of the one in charge...the one who has "been there...done that" and so is the wise one, the elder or the professional expert. This is our focus

on our evolvement, our mission, in this life. This would be the High Self You that has garnered all the knowledge and understanding from all of your experiences. You are the Elder.

The Protector/Gatekeeper Guide – This is the Self aspect that has experienced bravery and strength from all of our lives. This aspect is also strength from wisdom as well as the courage to stand up to anything. So do we feel the energy of a protector guide or the energy of insight and experience of a warrior's wisdom?

Healer/Doctor – Knowing how well the body can repair itself to perfect DNA, as the very act of Life Force itself, this is the self healer. And like in the example of Edgar Cayce who channeled healing entities and knowledge, we can call upon the Universe as well.

Joy Guide – This is the aspect of our inner child...our silly self. This aspect of our High Self knows "you'll laugh about this someday" kind of thinking and helps us to not take ourselves so seriously.

Runners – These Spirit Guides are said to help with finding things, getting things ready for us in our daily lives. Well, here is an interesting thought to ponder: Since time and space do not limit the non-physical world, this aspect of the High Self can be thought of as "going ahead" and making sure everything is in place before "you" get there...actually going ahead in time to pave the way, tell us where things are, etc.

<u>Helper/Teacher</u> – This is the cumulative knowledge of all lives lived that the High Self refers to.

Angels – A couple of Views

Angels have been documented in nearly all world religions over time. They are regarded as the vibration "closest to God" and in service to all. Traditional views are that angels do not incarnate as "regular people" but stay on the angel realm assist, guide and protect. Some say they are assigned at birth and others believe they are at our soul level, across all of our incarnations. Angels are available whenever we call upon them.

Colors

You can meditate on meeting your Spirit Guide. You can also meditate on an indication from your High Self on any aspect of you. In some cases, you will get a personification as referenced above, or you may get a feeling or a color. These can be related to the energies of the chakras, our energy centers, which also relate to our state of mind.

Just like a prism that separates white light, the chakras separate into the colors of red, orange, yellow, green, blue, indigo, and violet. These colors can be used as indicators of our focus. Reds are typically for survival and our physical needs; orange is our emotional balance to relation to others, yellow is our personal expression and power, green is related to love, and our emotional balance and our relationship to self, blue is communication and creativity, indigo is psychic awareness and vision, and purple (or white) is our spiritual connection. So as you meditate and see specific color or colors, you may consider that it relates to an area you are working on (fear or love, ego or oneness) or to gain information for your self.

Ultimately, you are always in control. You can believe in a Spirit Guide network if that works for you or a Spirit Team of One. There are no right and wrong ways to work with the Universe. This is just a different perspective to say "hey, it's just me" and feel right at home with who you already are and the loved ones on the Other Side.

And loved ones? Yes. We are not restricted to just working with Spirit Guides, just working with Angels, just working with St. Germaine, etc. We can have our loved ones in Spirit also available for guidance and support.

A young woman had given birth to her first child, a boy. When the baby was a month old, the family traveled to her parents' house for a visit. They stayed in one of the bedrooms, with the baby in a alcove area nearby. The mother woke up in the middle of the night to the sounds of her baby stirring, ready for a feeding. As she got up and walked into the alcove, she saw an image of a woman holding her baby in her arms, and comforting him. At first, she thought it was her own mom but soon realized that this woman was her deceased grandmother who had passed during her pregnancy. The woman laid the baby down into the crib, smiled at the young mother, and turned to walk away, vanishing into the end of the room. The young mother ran to the crib to find her baby comforted and sound asleep.

Our many readings constantly confirm the wonderful experiences of the Spirit around us, whether it is our High Self, our Spirit Guides, Angels or our loved ones. Why, then, would we need to protect ourselves when accessing this realm?

Chapter Eight

"Nothing in life is to be feared. It is only to be understood."
--Marie Currie

A Conversation about Protection – Can We Talk?

Susan: Six years after my mother's passing, I was driving with my eight year old daughter, who was sitting in the passenger seat next to me. As I was about to go through an intersection, a loud voice said "SUSAN!" coming from my right side, so I turned my head to look. At that moment, a large truck was barreling toward us and about to run the red light. After settling down, I turned to my daughter and said, "I'm so glad you said my name. You saved us. But why did you say 'Susan' and not 'mommy?' She looked curiously at me and said "but mommy, I never said anything. I didn't see the truck either." I knew at that moment that it was my mother who had saved us.

As we mentioned in the previous chapter on Spirit Guides, we do not feel there is a need for protection when connecting to the realm of our loved ones and Spirit.

It all goes back to "what's in your universe?" ...what you believe is the overall nature of things...both in a physical perspective and in a non-physical perspective. Our channel is a direct line from our self, to our High Self to Creator. If we are this direct line, there would not be a need for intermediaries, such as Spirit Guides, therefore there would not be a need for protection. It's not what's out there, spirit guide, ghost, attachment, etc....it's you and God.

Think of when you have had an experience of connecting to a loved one during a time going about your daily life, you didn't go into a trance, you didn't protect yourself, or any of that "medium stuff," it just happened! Spirit came in...they communicated...and they left.

So why would then it be necessary to "protect yourself" when doing this work on purpose? If the intention for readings is for loving guidance, healing, comfort, etc. why would anything negative be involved? There is no reason for these two things to be intertwined...accessing Spirit and opening the door to negativity. Spirit is you and God and that relationship is in your belief...love or fear...you choose.

The psychic medium is always in control of the environment in which he/she works. If there is fear of negative energies or entities "out there" when they open for communication, it will manifest! You can imagine the Cowardly Lion repeating over and over "I do believe in ghosts, I do believe in ghosts, I do I do I do" and he was terrified.

There are no negative entities "looking for our Light" to attach to; no "low vibration" spirit guides to hijack our readings and trick us into doing something we don't intend to do. If someone claims to hear their "spirit guides" telling them to do harm to themselves or others, we strongly advise medical intervention as this suggests an unhealthy mind.

A psychic-medium must make the choice to be in a loving state (or vibration) or a fearful state, when entering this work. We go in with the power of God's love...and that's pretty much it.

Generally speaking, if you feel you live a balanced and healthy life, this will reflect in your expression of Spirit.

What about psychic attacks or psychic vampires?

We knew you were going to ask that!!! You know the feeling you get if you found out that those around you were talking negatively about you, were angry at you or jealous, you would feel their energy change, especially in close contact. This is affecting your psyche, your conscious and sub-conscious mind, so when we interpret these feelings and energies negatively, we feel it is an attack. This can be referred to as a psychic (psyche) attack...but it does not mean that someone is getting into your mind and planting horrible thoughts or curses in you. If you explain experiences as psychic attacks, you may want to review your fears and past conditions so that they do not influence your life.

That's not to say we don't have opening prayer or statement, but it's to set the intention and attitude of the reading, bring confidence and comfort to the client, and go in with gratitude for the opportunity to serve. This is our opening, like your password to Spirit, for connection.

Engage

en·gage

verb

: to hire (someone) to perform a particular service : to pay for (help, services, etc.)

: to get and keep (someone's attention, interest, etc.)

: to start fighting against (an opponent) (*formal*)

Chapter Nine

"It is a process of diverting one's scattered forces into one powerful channel."

--James Allen

I see, I sense, I hear, oh my!

Everyone knows we have five physical senses that provide our brains signals of the environment around us and what we are doing in it. "Clair" means "clear" and refers to the process the mind uses to interpret signals from the non-physical world around us. You can think of E.S.P. as the non-physical side of each of our physical senses. The mind uses the "memory of" the input to garner information about an object, a person, a location or an event.

A list of the common clairs are:

Clairvoyance – clear seeing
Clairaudience – clear hearing
Clairsentience – clear feeling (empathic)
Clair cognizance – clear knowing
Clairgustance – clear tasting/smelling

Those mediums that would say "I see" ... would be considered clairvoyant. Clair, meaning clear, voyant meaning sight; clairvoyant means clear sight. You will hear mediums say "I see with my third eye" or "my second sight" or a "vision". Although some will see with their actual eyes, most do not.

To be clairvoyant in an intuitive way would simply be to see that which exists in your imagination. It is the memory of sight. The ability is to access and trust the pictures that your memory is showing you. An example might be if I say to you "close your eyes for just a moment and imagine a red rose." In your mind, you will see your memory of what a red rose looks like to you. You'll see it as deep red, long stem or short stem, full bloom or as a bud. If you took a snapshot of the red rose in your memory, it'll be different than everyone else in the room. So in essence, intuitive clairvoyance is the memory of sight.

When a medium says "I hear"... this would be considered clairaudience. This would be the ability to hear sounds which are not present to the physical ear. If I say to you, remember the song "Happy Birthday" you may hear that in your head without anyone actually singing it out loud to you. This is the memory of sound and this is intuitive clairaudience.

When a medium says "I feel", they would be considered clairsentience. We have all had moments in life when we feel another's pain or joy. Sometimes you actually feel it in your stomach area...or gut. A medium who feels would sense how a person passed physically or emotionally in their life or at the time of their passing. An example would be a person that passed with difficulty breathing, an intuitive clairsentient medium would know how that would physically feel without the actual physical discomforts or trauma. In other words, the medium is not experiencing an asthma attack to sense the shortness of breath. Our body's memory structure would bring us back to the memory of a time when we may have lost our breath or the emotions attached to that experience even if just seen on TV. The clairsentient medium also may receive personality traits of the deceased. They may experience their joys or difficulties in life given to the medium as memories of their own experiences within their emotions.

Clair cognizance is clear knowing and is the ability to know something without receiving it through normal or physical senses. You simply just know! There isn't a thought of knowing...it is just there. We have all experienced this, it usually is accompanied with the phrase, "I don't know why, but..." This is normal intuition. This type of intuition may be the easiest to understand because there is no actual stigma attached to it...people just say "I knew that!" and we say it with gusto!

Clairgustance is clear tasting and/or smelling (also referred to as clairalience). When the medium says "I'm smelling the scent of a cigar, the smoke is not actually in the air. The mind is recalling the memory of the cigar based on the cue from the loved on in Spirit. This is the same for taste. The medium may taste the favorite foods of the deceased, or even get a gag reflex of an undesirable taste.

The clair sense is a non-physical sense...a memory of the experience interpreted by the mind. The *direct* connection to a loved one in Spirit is not the function of a clair-sense but a case of physical Spirit contact! Yes, you heard that right!

- The mother that sees the deceased son, standing there looking healthy and well.
- Smelling the fleeting scent of a perfume worn by your mother who is standing by you.
- Hearing your dad call your name, "out of the blue" when he has been gone for many years.
- Knowing that the last time you saw a loved one alive was the last time you'd see them.

These are examples of actually experiencing your loved one who has passed, their Spirit.

Connie: When my mom passed, I started to smell cigarette smoke where I wouldn't normally smell it. I never picked up the habit, but as a medium knew this was a connection to my mom, who did have COPD later in life. My sisters, who do not regard mediumship as I do, were celebrating my sister's baby shower. One by one, they each came up to me to tell me of an incident of smelling cigarette smoke where there wouldn't normally be smoking. One sister returned from a vacation, and as she walked into her non-smoker home, she was greeted with "fresh cigarette smoke" not finding where it was coming from. Another sister would smell cigarette smoke "every Saturday, while doing laundry," and another smelled it "out of the blue" in her living room.

These incidents all happened with a couple of weeks of each other.

So you see you do not have to be a medium to experience Spirit...this is an everyday connection through your natural channel to your loved ones.

A Self Assessment:

This is a quick exercise to see how you receive thoughts (communication). Take a moment and look at one word at a time (use another sheet to cover the list as you go through it) and allow yourself 30 seconds to process this word. Notice how you take the information in. Do you see a picture of the word...do you remember how it would feel in your hand...can you smell something from it...can you taste something from it? Does this word invoke an emotional response from your body or memories?

Check all that apply for each word. Feel free to jot down any details that are associated with the word.

	See?	Smell?	Touch?	Emotion?	Memory?
Grapefruit					
Sand paper					
Cotton Ball					
The Beach					
Evergreen Tree					

Did you see three out of five of each item? You may be strongly clairvoyant.

Your ability to visualize the memory of sight is what would define as clairvoyant abilities.

Did you smell three out of five of each item? You may be strongly clairgustience.

Your ability to remember what something smells or tastes like without actually smelling or tasting is what defines clairgustient abilities.

Did you feel you can touch three out of five items without the item being in front of you? You may be strongly clairsentient. Your ability to feel that which is untouchable is what defines clairsentience.

Did you get an emotional response or a memory of an event for three out of five items? You may be strongly Clair cognizant or empathic. This would be described as someone who feels emotions from others or past memories, many times receiving it in the abdominal area of the body, otherwise known as the solar plexus. This is also known as a gut feeling.

If you checked several boxes across the board, without an actual pattern, you are strongly connected to all of your psychic senses! As you continue developing your psychic abilities, one or more of these senses may become stronger than the others.

CHAPTER TEN

"The greatest discovery of my generation is that human beings can alter their lives by altering their attitudes of mind."

--William James

Mediums and Psychics – Is it This or Is it That?

Mediumship is generally categorized into physical mediumship and mental mediumship. Physical mediumship is basically engaging spirit energy and experiencing it through the physical senses. Examples are:

- Ectoplasm – A supernatural viscous substance that is supposed to exude from the body of a medium during a spiritualistic trance and form the material for the manifestation of spirits.
- The movement of objects such as table tipping, Ouija (or spirit) board for guidance information
- Spoon-bending – bending metal objects (typically table wear) without physical force, or unusually less use of physical force.
- Automatic Writing, Direct Writing and Spirit Art – writing, journaling and artwork as a result of connecting with the High Self or others in the Spirit realm.
- Precipitated Spirit Art – When artwork appears on a canvas through the use of spirit energy, most times

through séance events. A noted pair were Elizabeth and Mary Bangs at the turn of the 20th century.

- Transfiguration – when spirit faces show up over the face of the medium
- Apports – the transference of an item from one place to another; or the appearance of an item from an unknown source
- Divination – This is using items to see images or get movement to interpret as information, such as Pendulums, Divining Rods, Crystal Balls, Scrying Mirrors, Tea Leaves.
- Orbs –Orbs are one of those things that have a lot of controversy. They can be explained as dust, water vapor, particles, bugs, or the physical manifestation of spirit energy. This is our two cents: Yes. There are times for one or all of these explanations. We've seen some pretty amazing orbs, complete with faces that defy any other explanation. So, the jury may be out, but we are in!

Mental mediumship is communication with spirit. Today, there are many names being used to describe the mental mediumship work. You may hear psychic, psychic-medium, clairvoyant, intuitive, medical intuitive, empath, sensitive, a channel, a trance channel, etc. They all describe various ways to connect to the unseen world from being very conscious to being in a deep, meditative state to receive and convey psychic and mediumistic information.

The title the medium uses may suggest a particular type of information they work in, such as a medical intuitive is a medium who works with the energies of the bodies, and can interpret the health of energy centers (referred to as chakras), organs or body systems.

Generally speaking, however, a medium by any name is a person who accesses information from the non-physical world. For example, if you were to come across these various titles in a psychic fair and are unclear as to their particular service, be sure to ask so that you get the type of reading you desire.

What is the Difference between Psychic and Medium?

We, as intuitive beings, reach toward another person in order to communicate and this is not always done with words or body language. Much of our communication is led by intuition. Words are not our only form of communication. We've all had those moments when we've communicated with another with just a look or a thought and later have been validated.

A popular saying in the divination world is: "All mediums are psychics but not all psychics are mediums." We do not agree. We are interpreting energy around us and around others and we learn to turn that into a conversation. Whether a person can only read energy from those living (psychic) or only read energy from those who have passed (medium), it is the choice of the person, not a restriction in the energy or a measure of expertise.

The type of information a psychic-medium will access will range from past to present to future. The future is sensing the energies that the client already has "in play" one way or another, consciously or not. For example, a person who has been given increased work duties may be up for a promotion. A medium may sense this and mention it as a future event. But the client's free will and choice is paramount and circumstances can change with a decision in a blink of an eye.

Predicting Death

This is a subject to be dealt with seriously and ethically. One of the main reasons people do not see a psychic-medium is because they "don't want to hear when they or someone else is going to die." Somehow, the role of a psychic-medium has been tainted as a messenger of death. But that is far from the case of today's professional psychic-medium.

The interpretation of the information received by the medium is on all levels...hearing, sensing, feeling, seeing, knowing...and that there is no "death" sense that can be clearly and definitively stated. It is similar to the death card in the Tarot that means transition from one thing to another, and not literally death of the physical body, but a change in any aspect of your life. Also, there is no benefit to the client to hear of their passing, which is a violation of their free will and choice.

The readings by psychics, mediums and psychic-mediums can vary so let's talk about psychic versus medium, in general:

Psychic:

We believe that all people are intuitive. That the world would not have survived without intuition...gut instinct...a hunch. So how would we describe the person that feels they have an extra sense, or an extra knowing? The common term would be to say they are psychic.

This may mean that this person is sensitive to the subtle energy that everyone possesses. The psychic person would actually receive information much like radio waves from another's personal energy. The psychic person can feel personal information such as emotions, physical sensations, as well as things that are relevant to the person's life at that moment.

This is because this information is stored in our personal energy field otherwise known as aura. The psychic person has the awareness and willingness to receive this type of information. This is where mind-reading comes in. Psychic is not reading another person's mind. If something is on your mind, it is in your aura and can be easily accessed by another. Some may argue much of this is the interpretation of physical cues, body language, etc. Psychic energy goes beyond the physical appearance and into the non-physical as information.

Medium:

To believe that you are a medium is to have an understanding that energy of life exists beyond the physical body...is eternal. A medium is someone who feels, senses, sees, or hears information from someone who has passed to the non-physical realm.

We've all heard the famous quote "I see dead people" but the senses and sensibilities would tell us that this is not always as clear cut as one would see in a Hollywood film.

In a medium conversation, we communicate with the energy of a Spirit or someone who has passed away, has deceased. They would communicate with us in order to help their loved ones to heal, bring comfort to them, validate, or to move forward in life. In a psychic conversation, we communicate with the energy of a living being, or life's energy. Either way, psychics and mediums are touching in with the energy of everything around us, existing in the physical and in the non-physical, through their senses.

CHAPTER ELEVEN

"All necessary truth is its own evidence."
--Ralph Waldo Emerson

The Conversation Begins with You

Why would someone seek out a psychic-medium and what value would the reading bring?

In our experience, the top 10 reasons might be:

1. Is my deceased loved one "ok" – Are they happy now?
2. Comfort – Did they suffer? Was there fear?
3. Closure – saying goodbye. "I wasn't there to say goodbye…"
4. Validation of things that have happened. "Was I just imagining that?"
5. Clarity around a passing, or how or why an accident or death happened. "Why did the car go off the road?"
6. If their loved one knows of the clients current life events. "Do they know we got married, had a child, etc."
7. Relationships – "Will I find love…is so-and-so good for me?"
8. Career – "I have an opportunity at work…should I take it?"

9. Solving an unfinished business – "Are they angry on how the estate was handled?"
10. Personal Growth/Journey – "Am I on the right path...am I doing the right things?"

A professional psychic-medium can provide answers to these types of questions. Through a clear connection to Spirit, the psychic-medium provides sincere evidence and messages, providing value and maintain the respect to the sitter. The reading is a service for the sitter, from the perspective of the sitter and not about the "great and powerful" medium and their connection to the unseen world.

The Psychic Reading

The psychic part of the psychic-medium deals with the energy of life, or living energy. Psyche means of the self, a derivative of the word psychic. The information is all about you, and it's about how you affect others and how they affect you. The psychic is not reading your mind, but rather interpreting the energy of your life, with all of his/her senses and communicating what is sensed back to you, the client.

A strong psychic reading would provide information, options, perspective and guidance to help the client move forward in a positive way. The psychic will connect to a personality trait of the client that validates them in a way to see opportunities ahead of them. The psychic reading offers another perspective of an issue so that client would see more options and avenues to take. Guidance, not instruction, is offered in a way that does not take away free will and choice. The client should leave the reading feeling empowered and uplifted.

For example, during a psychic fair, Sue overheard a fellow medium say to the client of the "long and hard road ahead." While the psychic may have clearly picked up the energy/information of the arduous time ahead for the client, the language used left her feeling defeated. This is weak language on the part of the reader. There is an interpretation of what is "long and hard" from one person to the next. Also, the phrasing used was a reflection of the reader's beliefs, filters and essentially, ego. The language of the strong psychic in this case would have been to say to the client "the strength that you will gain as you move this situation...." so that the reader acknowledges there is a challenge but that the client will rise above it to a positive end.

Another example of weak language of the psychic reader is bringing in ambiguous or eccentric information. By eccentric, we mean when the information shared is really coming from the belief system of the reader, and not the energy aura of the client.

A popular belief system is that of elementals (nature spirit) and totem animals. These are strong archetypes for the characteristics that we can call upon for guidance and strength. However, if a psychic begins to talk about either fairies or bear medicine and the client looks confused or befuddled, the psychic has not connected to the client, but to their own beliefs. The interpretation of the information is now useless...there is no value in this reading for the client.

The strong psychic may indeed feel fairy energy or bear medicine energy around the client. The conversation with the client to describe what this means must match the client's beliefs! The point here is that psychics receive this type of information all the time, but it is paramount that the conversation is in everyday language, something the typical person can walk away with.

In the case of receiving fairy or totem energies, the psychic may say "I feel a strong connection to nature, as in gardens and forests and that you may be missing that at this time." This type of information is typically symbolic, a way to garner the essence of the message for the client.

The strong psychic is also one that relies more on the sixth sense that the other five senses. This means that the strong psychic will go with intuition and not on a person's appearance, mannerism, smells or mood at the time of the sitting. For example, a professional man may show up at a reading, dressed casually that day, just pumped gas for his car and that last thing he needs hear is that he works on cars for a living.

A psychic-medium reading offers an opportunity to address a different perspective to aid in decisions, clarity and forward movement.

- When will I get married?
- When will I get a job?
- Will I have success in my life?
- Will I be ok after my divorce?
- Will my children be ok?

- Is this a choice I should make?
- Will I find love?
- Will my house sell?
- Should I move to (another town, city, state)?

A psychic reading should never take free will away, but will offer up alternatives, possibilities or choices that may or may not have been addressed so far. The psychic medium may not see the answer, but senses the energies of the potentiality. Wayne Dyer says "Change the way you look at things and the things you look at change." The reading, then, becomes a vehicle for introspection, for the person to look at what's going on inside to make a change on the outside.

The psychic reader occasionally may use various divination tools, which merely means to get in touch with the divineness in each of us...e.g., the High Self of us. These tools are means of focus and offers symbols that facilitate the dialogue/reading.

Samples of divination tools are:

- Tarot Cards – a structured 78 card deck that includes major and minor arcana and 4 suits
- Oracle Cards – a free-form art deck of cards, usually with inspirational message or key phrases
- Angel Cards – cards that will depict various angels and their guidance/messages

- Pendulum – a weight, usually metal or gemstone, that swings freely at the end of a string or chain, to answer yes/no type of questions
- Divining Rods – These are metal rods shaped in an "L" or sticks, originally used to find water, but can also link to the person's high self for yes/no types of questions
- Runes – a set of ancient symbols carved in a stone, tile, wood, etc., that have specific meanings in the layouts used
- Tea Leaves – this is the art of interpreting the shape/manner of tea leaves after the tea is consumed, that provide guidance/messages for the client.
- Palm Readings – This is a way to read and understanding the lines and lumps of a hand that will provide insight to the client.
- Crystal Ball / Scrying – This is a way to look at objects such as a crystal ball, a mirror or even clouds and interpreting the shapes and symbols into a reading of guidance and message.
- Throwing – This is where the reader with "throw" a grouping of objects such as crystals, bones, flower petals, etc., and interpreting the shapes and symbols into the reading.
- Spirit or Talking Board (commonly referred to as the brand name Ouija Board) – This is a flat board with letters and numbers and the person uses a planchette to spell out messages. This is addressed more in Chapter 16.

- Psychometry – The ability to "read" an object.

A little more about psychometry:

Psychometry is a Greek word for a measure of energy, or the gathering of information from touching or holding an object. A psychic or medium holds an object that belonged to either someone who has passed or is living, and receives information about the owner from the energy of the object.

The psychic-medium may pick up information about the owner or holder such as:

- Personality/Character
- When/Where Lived
- Age
- Name
- Method of passing
- Whether the item was a gift or inheritance

Divination tools are a great way to expand the source of information and make it personal for the client.

The Evidential Medium Reading

A medium reading is a conversation between a psychic-medium and the spirits or energies of people, both living (psychic) and deceased (medium). An *evidential* medium is one who relays information that can be substantiated or validated by the sitter to know who the Spirit is they are talking with.

The Conversation a.k.a The Reading

A medium is someone who sees, hears, feels and senses Spirit and communicates with them in all of those ways. It isn't one sense at a time; it can be an orchestra of information that comes through the medium's thoughts, emotions or physical body. Because of all the unique ways the information comes through, the medium must interpret very quickly what the spirit is telling them.

An analogy is like watching someone else's home movies where there was no dialogue or sound. The sitter would understand where they were, who everyone was, and what was happening. The medium watches the movie without knowing any of that information and needs to interpret what is being shown. The job of the medium is then to verbalize what they are hear, see, feel or sense in a way that the sitter understands.

So what do we mean when we say the medium is having a conversation? The conversation is between the medium and the spirit. The medium then relays the information clearly to the sitter.

As in a regular conversation between two people, there is an exchange of ideas clearly spoken so that the other person understands and can respond. The information exchange goes back and forth until the conversation is finished.

In a conversation with Spirit, there is an energy exchange that is picked up by the medium's senses (or the "clairs") and interpreted. For example, a spirit who would have spoken a different language than the medium would still be able to communicate because the energy exchange contains the essence of the message.

Let's go through a scenario. A client decides to have a reading, looking to connect with a loved one who has passed. The medium opens to the energy of the spirit and acknowledges the presence of the loved one. The conversation now begins. The medium "introduces" her/himself to the spirit and begins to relay the information that the spirit is giving them. This information would include the medium's perception of the spirit, such as friendly or aloof, happy, pessimistic, sweet or obnoxious. This is the medium's first impression as though they just met them in life. The medium's job is to now guide the conversation with the spirit to access more information. We call this going deeper for evidence that validates the spirit to the client.

The Evidence

Some of those points of evidence can be either regarding the sitter (psychic) or their loved ones who have passed (medium)...and most of the times, both.

<u>Personality Trait</u>

- Easy-going
- Happy-go-lucky
- Gentle / Kind / Compassionate
- Meek / Shy

- Quiet / Didn't speak a lot
- Talkative
- Creative / Artistic / Musical
- Classy or Down to Earth
- Intelligent / Simple
- Difficult to get along with
- Narrow minded – saw everything as black or white
- Unyielding / Stubborn / Inflexible / Strong willed
- Opinionated / Biased

Weak words and phrases for personality is when there are general descriptions used that are not enough on their own. For example, the medium may say "they were a happy person" which may fit the loved one well enough. The evidence gets stronger when the medium adds to it; such as, "they were a happy person when all of the family was around the dinner table" or "he was happiest when he was driving his vintage car."

<u>Appearance</u>

- Age or age range
- Hair – bald or full head of hair, how they wore their hair, etc.
- Weight – Large build or lean
- A strong facial feature – like a large nose, strong jaw
- A physical impairment, such as a limp, a lazy eye, etc.
- Cultural or Ethnic features, mannerisms, dress

- How did they dress...dressed for work, wear a uniform, wore a particular color for their job, etc.

Weak words or phrases would be "they were tall" or "older" or "younger" as they are in the perspective of the sitter and the client: A person who is 5'10" can be described as short or tall, depending on the sitter's or medium's point of view. It is important that the medium does not give personal opinions on describing physical features because they may find themselves offending the sitter. Beauty is in the eye of the beholder!

Evidence around their passing

- Age of either the deceased or the client
- How they passed – illness, accident, etc.
- Symptoms of their illness – such as heart, breathing, wheelchair, cane
- Where they passed – at home, hospital, etc.
- Memories from their funeral, burial, memorial
- Who was with them when they passed
- Who "met them on the Other Side"
- Things that were said before passing, at their bedside

When talking about evidence of passing, mediums will pass on the information as they receive it but the loved one is no longer feeling any pain, experiencing the act of dying itself, etc. Those in Spirit can describe events like watching a movie...they no longer feel physical pain, emotional distress or mental anxiety as once in life and it is important that the client knows this.

Family Events, Memories

- Birthdays, Anniversaries, Weddings, Graduations
- New babies
- Other Passings
- Vacations and vacation spots
- Family Picnics
- Holidays
- Family Photos
- Inside Family Jokes
- Family Home and Surroundings

Relationships

- Relationship of the client to the loved on in Spirit
- Names and Nick names
- The feel of the relationship...close, strained, distant, etc.
- Siblings and other members
- Pets
- Friends
- Other Family Members
- Inside Jokes
- Recounts of their relationship that results in a healing

The medium needs to be in an unbiased state to avoid bringing any residue into the reading; for example, if the medium that had an issue with their alcoholic father must be mindful so that all fathers from readings wouldn't be alcoholic, abusive, difficult, drinkers, etc.

Hobbies, Occupations, Jobs

- Hobbies, Jobs, Occupations of either the client or the loved one.
- Type of workplace – office, construction, hospital, car
- Type of work –
- How they Dressed
- The emotion attached to their work or hobby
- Coworkers
- Timeframe – when they worked, how long they worked, retired, etc.
- Likes and Dislikes
- School / Education

Evidence comes from Spirit, the loved one who has passed, and is interpreted through the medium. When evidence is eccentric, or leaves the client confused and befuddled, it is most likely again from the medium, and not Spirit.

The Ethics and Responsibilities

There are many reasons a person sees a psychic-medium which can range from "just for fun" to being in a vulnerable state. In these cases, people are looking for closure, comfort or validation to move forward in their lives. For this reason, the medium has a great responsibility to the quality and excellence of the service, and more importantly, to "do no harm" to the client. We say "leave them better than you found them." A client should never leave a reading feeling fearful, paranoid, disempowered or guilty.

There is no governing body for psychic-mediums. It then becomes vital that the psychic-medium self-regulates to a level of professional and ethical work. There are certifications through organizations and religious institutions, but the medium is still responsible for the ethical service they provide.

The ethics and responsibilities of the professional mediums include:

- Free will and choice – ALWAYS maintain it!
- Confidentiality – This is similar to a doctor-patient agreement...what is said in the reading stays in the reading!
- Value – Significant evidence and messages
- Honesty – to be a clear channel for Spirit without any personal bias or judgment.

Whatever you call your self and your service, be honest about it to your clients. Psychics and mediums have people's lives in their hands and ethics and responsibilities are vital! When a psychic-medium has a grieving mother as a client and says they have connected with their child who has passed but all they say is that the child "was an old soul and understands why he/she left so early," you are not a medium or a psychic! You are a philosopher of metaphysical and spiritual studies as there was no evidence of connecting with the loved one on the Other Side. Ethics is also honesty of the medium and the reading service advertised and delivered.

The reading is communication, and valuable communication is using language that the client can clearly understand. It is supported by comprehensible evidence and realistic phrasing that is meaningful for the client. The professional psychic-medium, working on behalf of Spirit AND the client, strives to provide a high-quality, ethical service. While there are no licensing or governing rules, the substantiation of the professional shows up as a highly referred psychic-medium.

Chapter Twelve

"The only way to have a friend is to be one."
–Ralph Waldo Emerson

For You Sensitive Folks

What do we mean by that?

Sensitive people naturally feel the people and environment around them. They easily take on emotions from one person or a group of people. The person who is sensitive may initially be considered by others as unsocialable, dramatic, too emotional, or an outcast. In large crowds, the emotions can be very overwhelming to the point of the need to leave. We usually call sensitive people empathic, having the ability to feel others through emotions, and others' emotions.

If you feel you are an empath, know that it's a matter of understanding and control. An empath's interpretation of energy comes through their emotional sense and body sensations. An empath may cry suddenly, may feel overwhelmed, or everything is against them, experience unexplainable mood swings and may find themselves pulling away from others. Young children who are empathic may feel like an outcast as well, and develop withdrawing behaviors.

Because of this, taking in the emotions from a large crowd or a stressful environment can feel daunting, and can take a toll on a person's emotional state.

If you experience empathic sensations, here are a few examples and suggestions to work through them:

Example: You were excited to go to a party. You walked into a room full of people, feeling happy and suddenly being overwhelmed with a sense of sadness, dread, anxiety or anger.

In extreme cases of emotions from everyone in the room, such as very happy or very sad, the empath feels more of the energy of the emotion, but may not be able to discern what is "happy" or "sad". What you can do is to take a moment and go to a private area, like a hallway, and remember, the emotional state you felt (being happy and excited) before you walked into the room. Relax and quiet yourself and allow the emotions that you picked up, are not yours, to dissipate from you. You can repeat an affirmation such as "this is not mine, I release it and let it go."

Example: You feel you cry all the time...friends and family "roll their eyes" when you shed a tear because they do not understand why.

This again is a result of a rush of energies from others, and your reaction to it. Again, remember your happier state of being (mind and body) to regain your balance and emotional control. Don't be hard on yourself for being this way, just be aware and adjust accordingly. You are always in control!

There are beliefs that a highly sensitive person needs to "protect" themselves from the energies. This is sometimes associated with negative energies and one would need things like shields, bubbles, or mirrors to bounce the energy off of them.

We do not agree, primarily because this places the empath as a victim, and in a powerless position. The power of the mind-body and intention serves the empath and/or the empathic medium. We can manage energies for intending and manifesting, and this would be the same thing to manage energies of your surroundings. Energy creates...or you react...you choose.

The Empathic Medium

As an empathic medium, you may feel the extremes of physical, mental and emotional sensations, whether you are doing a reading or investigating paranormal activity in a building. The empathic medium must develop a strong sense of self and balance to discern these extremes of emotions and feelings.

Susan: I was asked to go to a home to investigate strange and unexplained noises. I arrived to this home to hear pounding coming from the second floor. I immediately went toward the sound, which sounded like a bowling ball being rolled on a wooden floor. However, when I got to the second floor, it was wall-to-wall carpeting so the sound made no sense. I entered the master bedroom at the end of the long hallway and was met with a cool breath to my face, smelling of vodka, which I confirmed with the house occupants was not coming from them. Then I immediately felt aggressiveness, and the feeling of being a woman dominated by a strong man, which made me angry as well. I asked out loud "Who are you and why are you trying to bully me?" The response was from a man in spirit, named Joseph, who showed me working in a metal foundry type setting and a rail car. He told me he was an alcoholic and abusive to his wife, who passed before him. Because of this abusive behavior, he felt he was doomed to hell. At that point, I told him he was already a spirit ready to return home to the love and healing of God. I felt resistance but told him of a young woman waiting for him to take his hand. This turned out to be his younger sister who passed 65 years earlier. I felt he left the house, which was reported later to be much lighter and quiet.

During the reading, in order to maintain your professionalism and especially the respect of the client, you must also be discerning with your words.

For example, the empathic medium may see an infant in the arms of a loved one in Spirit. You may feel abdominal pain, heartache, may sense blood, and severe emotional anguish. In order to convey this information to your client you may say "I'm feeling there was sadness attached to the loss of a child that the child came too early into this life. The situation may have been a crisis for the mother's well being. While the loss of this child is very sad, I'm being shown it being cared for by a loved one in Spirit." The empathic medium needs to understand to put these feelings into words that are comforting and loving to the client. This is very important!

The medium needs to understand and make it understood that there is no suffering in the spirit world. All information that the medium receives is a means of identification of the loved one in Spirit and works through the medium in their way, even as perhaps by accessing memories of that medium to use as frame of reference.

Many times, even before a person realizes they are an "empathic medium" they may already work in the energy healing arts. The channel for healing is the same channel for spirit communication (as well as prayer, or guidance from our High Self), and can be helpful to the medium. The energy healer is adept at recognizing changes in energies along the body or chakra centers. So the empathic medium can garner information from Spirit by asking "if I were doing a healing on you, where would I be focusing on?" The information from Spirit can provide method of passing, illnesses endured later in life, injuries incurred from a fall or accident, etc.

All people can feel the energies around them, in one way or another, whether you are a professional psychic-medium or not. It boils down to how you interpret (action) and you handle (reaction) each situation.

Chapter Thirteen

"True happiness involves the full use of one's powers and talents."
--John W. Gardner

Meditation: Om.....Amen

There are so many different reasons to meditate. Some people do it to relax, for religious or spiritual reasons, for health, as well as to connect to Spirit. The belief is to "go within" that would be to lower your brainwave activity to access the High Self and God-ness.

There are a couple of common sayings about meditation and prayer: Prayer is talking to God; meditation is listening to God; or meditation is prayer, prayer is meditation. Many people would pray to ask for guidance, release stresses and anxieties, surrender. So when someone meditates on a rosary or prayer beads, it is focus and intention to release, go within...get to the channel...go to Source.

While it is beneficial in many ways to meditate, it is not necessary to do to receive information from Spirit.

Dom F. lost a dear friend to a drug overdose at the age of 24. This young man loved to wear large plaid shirts. The week after his friend's passing, Dom was in his room watching TV when he noticed something out of the corner of his eye. When he turned to look, he saw the image of the plaid shirt walking out of his room. He jumped up to see more but no one was there. While he was startled and his heart raced, he felt a great peace come over him. He knew without a doubt it was his good friend.

If you compare your brain to a computer system, meditating would be like clearing the cookies, or clearing the cache, to get rid of unwanted information. If you have had a stressful day, it would make sense to go through a clearing process, such as a brief meditation, to clear your mind. A clear mind is a clear channel, and a clear channel can pick up and interpret information easily and evidently.

The closing of the eyes already puts the brain on "slow down" mode. The aid of listening to bi-neural beat music to sync up the right and left hemispheres of the brain is also helpful to get to the meditative state. People will attend churches, sacred services, rituals, or set up their own sacred space, to get in the mood...light incense, candles, play chanting or meditative music. But the important thing is to do whatever you feel relaxes you.

It might be helpful to understand what the brain is doing in our various states of awareness. Normal brainwave activity runs at approximately 13-40 Hz. This is called the Beta state, and is our everyday thinking state, fully conscious of our environment, body and time.

When we begin to relax, closing our eyes and taking deep breaths, we enter a light meditative state, and the brain slows to 7-13 Hz, this is the Alpha state. We are still conscious but the mind begins to quiet and we are not as aware of the world around us. An interesting fact is that alpha waves do not appear until three years of age.

The next state is the Theta state, which is 4-7 Hz. It is that state of consciousness between wake and sleep. It is believed that a psychic connection occurs when the brainwaves are slowed to the Theta state. Typical experiences here are hearing your name, feeling as though you are being touched, being held down (sleep paralysis), sitting on your bed or breathing on your face. This occurs because you are in the state of complete relaxation and the brain filters are not engaged to block out these connections. When you awaken, most times fight-or-flight instincts have engaged and what you feel is fear...but you were just startled.

The last state is Delta, where we are completely unconscious and in a deep restorative sleep. The brain slows to 0-4 Hz.

There is evidence to support the state of brain activity to the acts of deep relaxation and transcendental meditation and the connection to Oneness consciousness. What we have found, however, that despite these states of meditation or brain activity, most people have psychic experiences that happen in the middle of the day, while going about their normal activity. We can sense, feel and experience energy of people, places and things around us any time and in any brain state of consciousness. Accessing the information from this energy exchange can be a voluntary or involuntary sense.

Most psychic-mediums do have a practice of meditation as part of their natural balance of mind, body and spirit, whether it is through chanting or prayer. The preparation a psychic-medium performs is to get to a state of relaxation and balance, not to match brainwave frequencies of psychic-medium information. This sets up a clear channel for the psychic-medium to receive evidence and messages, without the clutter of their mind and influence of their filters, to provide the best possible reading and service to the client.

Experience

ex·pe·ri·ence

noun

: the process of doing and seeing things and of having things happen to you

: skill or knowledge that you get by doing something

: the length of time that you have spent doing something (such as a particular job)

CHAPTER FOURTEEN

"You and I do not see things as they are.
We see things as we are.

--Herb Cohen

Mediums are Real Characters!

A dialogue with those who have passed can be as regular as our everyday conversations between two people. The reading is a conversation between three people, but the medium is two people in one.

Spirit does not provide information that will not ring true with the client, but the medium can! The medium, when allowing their beliefs, filters and personal philosophies to dominate the incoming information and message, can color the reading. In other words, the characteristics of the medium can influence or portray the reading given.

The reading includes evidence and messages from spirit. Evidence is information directly from loved ones who have passed that prove to the sitter that the spirit is present. Information such as how they passed, what they did for a living or personal traits or characteristics. The message can be comfort, validation, perspective or even just a hello. The messages may not be profoundly deep or life-changing guidance, but in all cases, the message will be the "icing on the cake" and clearly identifiable from the person with whom the medium is conversing.

We've thought of several "characteristics" of mediums and how each type is unique and may use different techniques and personal strengths to connect to Spirit and provide a reading service. These are just an idea of how our differences may show up in our reading styles.

The Professional Medium

As a baseline, anyone who receives information from spirit and conveys it to another ~~takes~~ becomes a professional medium and takes on the ethics and responsibility of the work. This does not matter whether you charge a fee or not. As in any other profession, a great deal of training, practice and experience makes for the professional medium and you are accountable for the quality of the service.

Let's put this in business terms...the product, the service and the brand. The reading is the service as well as the product. The medium is the product as well as the brand. How the medium, then decides to create their brand and create their product/service is what would determine the degree of professionalism.

The Evidential Medium

The Evidential Medium is one who connects to Spirit and communicates back to their client with clear, concise information regarding the loved one passed that the client can understand fully. This medium truly proves the continuity of life, that the energy of Spirit can be engaged and communicated with. For those seeking validation, comfort, closure, and true contact with their loved one, we believe this to be the strongest characteristic of any psychic-medium.

The Empathic Medium

To experience mediumship from an empathic point of view would be to feel information in your body, and understand it emotionally or mentally. When connecting with a spirit, the empathic medium may feel physical sensations associated with the passing of the person. Some examples may be pressure in the chest, nausea, head pain or even the sense of panic. The job of the empathic medium is then to convey these sensations or feelings verbally to the sitter. We may also experience mental or emotional states, such as confusion, sadness, relief, depression, manic and off-balance states, mental illness and chemical or alcohol impairment. We may experience the feelings of guilt, compassion, love, or distaste. In order to not experience the negative side of these feelings, I had to understand how my mediumship works and they these are not my conditions. This allows the empathic medium to release these sensations they feel from others and Spirit and still do the reading.

The Left-Brain Medium

The left-brain medium is one who may have to make sense of everything they feel, hear, see or experience through Spirit in order to know "what to do with it." They know mediumship is an ability they can learn and expand upon and thus it is through assessment and practice that helps the left-brain medium increases their understanding of Spirit. A left brain medium may experience one sense more active than another and that is something left-brainers need to be ok with, as we tend to have an "all or nothing" attitude about learning. The abstract nature of receiving symbolic information may "overload" the assessment process as they search for a logical and organized approach to it all.

Typically, left-brainers are spending a lot of brain power on assessing and processing. This puts the left brain in the beta state, the conscious thinking state, so to quiet the processing brain so input from Spirit can be easier to receive, the left brain medium may wish to engage in a meditation practice, or some deliberate set-up of quiet and centeredness. It may not need to be hours, but most likely several minutes to settle and receive.

Another way a left-brain medium makes and keeps a link to spirit is to engage the right brain, which is the imagination/intuitive brain. This may be done by journaling, doodling, spirit art, scrying, listening to chanting music, etc., which are examples of right brain activities.

Other ways to help a left-brain medium,

...follow a set-up routine to purposefully relax and release the busyness of the day

...consider the power of focusing on the breath, telling the mind that is the signal to center, and return to deliberate breathing anytime during the reading should the medium feel sluggish or not connected.

...work on the strengths of mediumship and not the number of weaknesses

...not to over think or over assess during the reading. Let it flow. Use a journal to garner the wisdom of the reading process later

Then, like all mediums, trust the rest of the reading.

The Religious/Spiritual Medium

The religious medium is governed by a specific belief system and would have a varied viewpoint.

1. This medium would bring their religious rules and guidelines into their reading. They may cite specific passages or understanding as a part of their religion.
2. The medium who would have self imposed rules or boundaries set forth by their spiritual belief system but not governed by a specific doctrine. For example, a Medium may be "Christ-based" in belief but not carry any particular Christian beliefs into the reading.
3. The medium who may express the information through religious verse and psalm.
4. The medium that calls on specific saints in their work.

The Spiritual Counseling Medium

We believe this is a loosely used term. Spiritual counseling can be termed as a medium that helps their client to connect to their own spirituality. Many mediums take on this name in order to give advice through psychic means. Unless you are licensed to be a counselor or therapist, use caution when putting this on your card. All mediums receive information from Spirit that could be deemed guidance but by no means should be confused with counseling. Check the laws in your area. Food for thought.

The Spirit Artist

There may be a couple of ways to describe spirit art. A medium may be inspired to "just draw, paint or color" before, during or after a reading. The medium is touching in through clair cognizance and expressing through imagination on paper to capture the essence the loved one passed. An example might be the medium drawing objects, layouts of a room, animals, and other evidences of the life lived. Another way a medium uses spirit art is through conscious choice; for example, the medium may go into a reading with the expressed purpose of drawing the loved one in spirit. This would be a spirit portrait.

The Angel Medium

There are a couple of ways to consider what angel readings are. The angel medium believes angels play an important role in their daily life and therefore will offer the reading from the perspective of unconditional love, comfort and guidance, words of hope to the client. The medium's understanding of the angelic realm offers the power of angel's guidance for the sitter to make their own decisions as they move forward. The angels will not interfere with free will and choice, and the medium is well aware of that.

Angel card readings, using tarot or oracle cards, is a psychic reading that uses the interpretation of the artwork and key words to offer the guidance, empowerment and comfort. The intuitive angel card reader will also bring in loved ones who have passed, making a mediumistic connection.

The Healing Medium

All mediums are healing mediums. Energy healing work is the intention of having a higher power focused by the healer for the benefit of the client. For example some of the brand names are Reiki, Integrated Energy Therapy, Energy Medicine, Emotional Freedom Technique, etc., but it is all included under the umbrella of energy healing. Ultimately, the channel that flows from our self to the Divine and used for communication is the same channel used for healing energies. When working, some healers receive guidance, bits of information that are not part of the healing but do pertain to the client. This is natural. However, it is then up to the healer/medium to state that as part of their healing service and let the client give permission to receive information as appropriate.

The Card Medium

The cards (tarot, oracle, and angel) are a divination tool for psychic energy. Cards and card spreads engage the imagination of the medium. They show a picture or blueprint of the psychic message and works with intuition of the psychic-medium. Cards offer tangible pieces of evidence for both the medium and client to see, understand and interpret the message and guidance offered. Tapping into that psychic energy, with Spirit involved, medium messages as well as psychic messages can be given and received through the cards. Always working with the

Source...there is no power in the cards, they are pictures on the table.

The Divination Medium

Types of divination include palm, pendulums, runes, crystals, scrying, bones, tea leaves, mirror, candles, etc.

As in cards, these are focusing tools. The medium will "know the source" of what the tool is saying to them, what the cards represent, what the bones say, what the candle is doing. These various tools will draw attention to key messages that the medium will offer...there is no power manipulating the cards, bones, etc.

The "Dear One" Medium

This is said to be a medium that channels entities other than loved ones who have passed. Channeling is a form of mediumship, receiving information that cannot be validated but is for the greater good of mankind. Very often, theses messages begin with the greeting "Dear Ones."

Another definition of channeling is when a medium connects to a spirit of a loved one and the medium allows the spirit to enter their voice and body to bring the message to the client. An example of this is in the movie, "Ghost", where Whoopie Goldberg channels Patrick Swayse's character in a séance.

The Sweetheart Medium

Every medium (person, really) has filters they see their world through. An optimist, a romantic, an idealist, will see the world through rose colored glasses in any situation. The well-meaning sweetheart medium may be uncomfortable with undesirable situations and emotions, such as ways of passing, the grief of the client, abuse, death of a child, anger or depression, etc. These may be considered "negative" by the medium who may avoid them to focus on positive aspects of the client's life. While these readings still offer value to the client, these types of readings may not touch deep enough for the sitter to receive the full potential of a healing.

The Color/Aura Medium

This medium sees or senses energy or aura around people, places and things. They may see energy as waves, like heat rising from the pavement on a hot day. Sometimes this will be in colors. This medium learns to attach color to an emotion, a physical sensation, or ailment. Each color will have a meaning to the medium who will usually describe the color's characteristics (also referred to chakras) along with the message, for example, red may describe a person's passion where yellow may describe their perkiness. They may also see colors surrounding the body. For example, the medium sees a vibrant green emanating from the chest of the sitter. This may describe the person as being very giving, nurturing, kind and loving.

The Paranormal Medium

The paranormal medium is a specialized service provider. These mediums are typically called into places that are believed to have physical spiritual activity. They may work with "ghost-busting" groups or by themselves.

The medium will have a dialogue with the spirit in the location and ask:

- Who are you?
- Why are you here?
- What do you want or need?
- Is there something you want to say?
- How can I help you?

Additionally, the paranormal medium is usually a strong medium that does much with psychometry, or gaining information from touch. Because much of the energy is believed to be stored in the physical location, these mediums will get information from the building itself; i.e., "if these walls could talk"...well they can! The paranormal medium may also be tasked with healing or cleansing the area.

The "Disclaimer" Medium

Faith and confidence is another key factor in mediumship. When either one is "threatened" by the fear of the medium or the "uncooperative" client, the disclaimer medium appears. These disclaimers discount the quality and value of the reading. You may hear mediums say:

- "I don't know what this means, but..."
- "I've only been doing this for a short time, so..."
- "I don't charge for my mediumship and I usually only do this for friends and family, but ..."
- "If you do not know who this is (in Spirit), it must be your Spirit Guide"

- "I can't make a connection...You must be blocking me, there is a negative energy around you, the moon in is Pisces...

A medium is a communicator. And just like in everyday conversations, there may be misinterpretations. The disclaimer medium will make excuses for not understanding what Spirit is offering them. The confident medium acknowledges any misinterpretations, and does their best to clarify further with Spirit.

A couple of more characters...

The Ninja Medium

According to Wikipedia, "a ninja was a covert agent or mercenary in feudal Japan. The functions of the ninja included espionage, sabotage, infiltration, and assassination, and open combat in certain situations." In this case, this is a medium who:

- Confronts you when not asked or invited
- Gives you information that is frightening without explanation
- Who leaves the client feeling vulnerable
- Who takes away the client's free will and choice
- Who may be egotistical...and describe their "readings and messages" with the slant of jealously, resentment, cynicism, pessimism, etc.

The "Oz" Medium

A reading is not the place to show off, to give messages in a superlative sense. The reading is for the benefit of the sitter, not the medium. With the Oz medium, you may hear:

- "I am so glad you came to me."
- "I've had this gift all my life and ..."
- "If you listen to me..."
- "Here's what you need (should) do..."

This medium may "talk the talk" but not walk the talk...meaning, they say all the right, loving, positive, words but their connection is to ego, not Spirit. This medium may leave you feeling that they are above you, that only they can help you (totally taking your free will). If the medium you experienced leaves you walking away feeling what they essentially said was how "great and powerful" they were, you were just hit by the Oz medium! *P.S.: The Oz Medium and the Ninja Medium are friends.*

The "Snake Oil" Medium

Wants to sell you stuff...keep you coming back..." "You have a dark energy/entity attached to you...for $350, I can take that away..." another $50, I can meditate on that and continue the reading"... and will usually suggest returning within a short period of time to become dependent on them or their guidance.

An ethical medium will have repeat customers, but suggest to their clients to return after 6-12 months, unless a different or specific situation comes up in the meantime. This maintains the free will and choice and personal power of the client.

Chapter Fifteen

"There is always a best way of doing everything..."
–Ralph Waldo Emerson

The Private Eye on the Medium

There seems to be a misguided perception due to TV shows, movies, about psychic-mediums walking up to anybody at anytime and sharing information they receive from Spirit.

When you see this on a TV show, understand that this is not as spontaneous as it appears to be. The person being read for has been asked for their permission in doing so and has signed waivers releasing the medium and the production company from any liability. Then the cameras roll!

This is something to bear in mind when you begin your psychic-medium development. Just because you can, doesn't mean you should! You may be walking through a store or other public place and feel as though you receive information regarding personal issues of a stranger, or their loved ones coming through from Spirit. To just walk up to them and offer this information is truly an invasion of their privacy. You have not been given permission to enter their personal space or their lives. It would be the same as walking up to a perfect stranger, without permission, hugging them and giving a kiss on the cheek. It's great to offer a hug, but a little creepy from a perfect stranger, isn't it?

Although you may feel this information is important, and you clearly heard it from Spirit, there is still a level of responsibility and respect for the individual and their free will and choice in their lives. You have no idea about this person's emotional or mental state of the mind, or how their day is going, or what their religious or cultural beliefs are.

People have beliefs that those in contact or connection with the spiritual realm would represent the devil, and messages may be misinterpreted, or the very thought of being a party to that realm may be very unsettling.

When you pick up a strong message for a stranger, and feel the need to take action, remember that the client is the one served. If you find yourself saying: "I felt/heard/saw this...I have to tell them that...I have to make sure..." reveals there is more "I" there than the client. If you must do something with this information, go home and journal it. You do not need to know you are right...you do not need to invade someone else's life in order to do what you think is your life calling.

Susan: A woman, Carol, who lives in another state, was shopping at a store when a woman came up to her and introduced herself as a psychic-medium. The medium said to Carol, "I have something very important to tell you and you need to listen carefully. I see a woman with you and she keeps saying the name Brian. Brian is in imminent danger and he needs to stay clear of fire, that I see him in fire, burned and that it would end him."

Carol thought long and hard about what this meant and who it may be for as she couldn't think of who Brian might be. She thanked the woman and said she would pass on the message to whomever it made sense for. The medium walked away feeling proud to have given the message she was carrying.

When Carol went home, she spoke to her neighbor and found that her neighbor's nephew was named Brian and so Carol passed on the information the medium had given her. Now there is a chain of information and this story is growing, like playing the telephone game. Brian's mother was in a complete panic state, and because of this information wouldn't allow Brian to attend summer camp.

Carol called me and asked if her neighbor's nephew was in danger of being burned in a fire. As a medium, I went in to ask and felt that the information was not literal, but symbolic, and that the boy was suffering from mental/emotional imbalance and the fire represented flare ups of anger and emotional distress.

After many months, Carol called me to let me know how things turned out. Brian, a 12 year old boy, was in the process of a diagnosis for bi-polar disorder. The fire would have been a symbol of his emotional/mental state since Brian was afraid of fire and would never go near it. This happened many years ago and today, this young man is fine. The information the medium received may have just been in symbolic terms.

The medium did not have control of her ego or her mediumship, as she felt it necessary to give a message without being invited to do so. Instead of helping the client, the medium's message created a panic that was of no value or service.

What about friends?

Privacy regarding mediums and friends goes in two directions: One from the medium to their friend and the other from the friend to the medium.

A medium in control of their mediumship would not impose on anyone, including their friends, without first asking for permission. Mediums may pick up on psychic and medium energies when with their friends, and the medium is also aware of what their friends are going through, so it may be easy to want to offer assistance. If assistance isn't requested, it is just an opinion and opinions are like toothbrushes...everybody has one but you don't want to use anyone else's.

The other side is that psychic-mediums require privacy too, and may not "on" 24/7. Friends who ask their psychic-friend "what do you see or hear for me?" are imposing on the psychic-medium's privacy. The psychic-medium is not at work, and their time off should be respected, like any other professional.

Another privacy matter is in regards to information the psychic-medium receives in general. Professional psychic-mediums should maintain the confidence of their clients and not divulge details of their private lives to anyone else.

The privacy issue should not be regarded lightly and is an ethical standard that is a part of the service, whether a psychic-medium practices professionally or not.

CHAPTER SIXTEEN

"A barrier is of ideas, not of things."

--Mark Caine

Addressing the Fears and Myths

There are many fears and myths around psychic phenomena and mediumship. Through the ages, the fear of the unknown and the need to create myths to make sense of things unseen is still apparent even in this modern age of quantum physics, intellect and free-thinking religion. It is very easy to continue a fear or myth regarding psychic-mediumship until the time it is addressed in the light of the day, and you have a chance to ponder the possibility of another explanation.

First you need to understand that a connection with your psychic self is only a connection with your self. You are not reaching into a mysterious void. This psychic connection is an inherent sense of being human...it is natural to be intuitive or to have intuition. The phrase "psychic connection" is just another term for natural intuition. How you develop that intuition depends on a number of factors, such as, the environment you were brought up in as a child, your own level of perceptions and interpretations from psychic experiences and the level of education and understanding you are receiving on the matter. You, or others around you, may have drawn conclusions (a.k.a. beliefs) from "negative" experiences or situations in the past. There are many places teaching psychic-medium studies that still carry a level of doctrine and principles that reflect some of the age-old myths and underlying fears.

Let's address some here. Below are various fears and myths, following by our understanding of the matter:

Fear: "Opening" to psychic or intuitive abilities opens the door to a place of unknown danger and negative energies.

Understanding: For the longest time in human history, there was a fear that the Earth was flat and prevented ship captains and explorers from going beyond a belief-imposed barrier. When that barrier was exposed and eliminated, the world was investigated, surveyed and open for travelers all over. So this fear of the unknown place of unseen energies and entities is probably the most popular and needs to be addressed on a couple of levels.

There are various religious and cultural beliefs that accessing the underworld, hell or the realm of lost souls will expose yourself to demons, dark angels, or harmful spirits (ghosts) or energies that will attach themselves to you and negatively affect your life. This is also repeated in games such as the Ouija Board, as well as in TV shows and movies.

The realm of the non-physical world is a mirror of your physical world and beliefs. If you believe that there is Heaven and Hell, or a plane of existence that should not be accessed, your conversations will incline to describe the world in that way. You may go into your psychic-medium studies with various "counter measures" to dispel negativity, such as surrounding yourself with mirrors, holding onto a particular crystal or amulet. In a sense, this is keeping the fear and relying on practices and ritual to safely connect and enter.

Don't put more power in the thing than the person holding it!

A belief in the pure love and joy of Source allows the possibility that Heaven is all around us, and with this understanding, you connect safely and confidently. You may have a prayer or ritual to begin your work and that is perfectly fine, but it is the power of your intention and understanding that guide you in your work.

Fear: Using an Ouija Board will open portals to demonic entities.

Understanding: Ouija is a brand name for an old Spiritualist parlor game, known as the spirit or talking board. It was developed in the height of the Spiritualist movement as a way for mainstream America to safely connect to loved ones who have passed. The power is not in the cardboard or the plastic; it's in the intention of the user. It works with kinetic energy...the energy of those on the board. Keep in mind that young teens have the most kinetic energy, so experiences would be erratic to say the least. Hollywood would have us belief that it is a dangerous tool, when in fact it is nothing more than cardboard and plastic.

Fear: Enhancing your psychic intuition is against my religious beliefs.

Understanding: If you are afraid that enhancing your psychic intuition is against your religious beliefs, you probably wouldn't be reading this book. So you may have questions on how being psychic and religion get along. Think about it this way, to understand our being on a soul level is acknowledging there is a higher power, beyond that of this physical life. Why then would it be considered against God if we are seeking to understand Unconditional Love and our relationship to Him/Her?

Fear: Being "out of control" of one's faculties and lack of choice.

Understanding: We believe that the Universal Law of Free Will and Choice puts us in control at all times. We would not be here if there was an element of victim-ness or a place in existence that we would stumble upon and be lost forever. Unlike TV and in the movies, nothing in the non-physical will harm you ...unless you allow it. This then speaks to the importance of your mental, emotional and physical health and being in balance. If you are in a place of good health or a loving heart, any psychic energy will be reflected accordingly.

Fear: Being physically touched or objects being moved or thrown around the room.

Understanding: When hearing people speak of spirits telling them to do harm to self and others, this is a reflection of their own imbalances. There is also a term called telekinesis or now referred to as psycho kinesis in which emotional/mental influence can affect physical systems and objects. This is more likely to explain various psychic experiences than a poltergeist or angry spirit. Energy is motion, so understand with a lot of energy, we can do stuff without intending to. When these types of things happen, assess what is going on emotionally and/or mentally with those involved.

Myth: Being psychic means reading minds.

Understanding: A psychic can pick up energies and thoughts disbursed in our energies...not necessarily all thoughts in your head. In other words, these thoughts are expended out as energies and we pick up energies. So if you and a friend are thinking along the same lines on a particular topic, you may feel you are reading the thoughts in their mind...but you may have picked up the energy of it. Moreover, psychics and empaths are picking up feelings rather than what you are doing later in the evening!

Fear: Being psychic/being with a psychic invades your privacy or the privacy of others.

Understanding: The origin of the word "psychic" comes from the Greek word, *psychikos*, which means of the soul. Our definition of it refers to connecting to that which cannot be seen is sometimes referred to as Spirit or energies pulled out of "the ethers". The information interpreted through a psychic or psychic-medium can be said to be soul to soul. "Thoughts are things" and someone who is sensitive to the energies/vibrations of others may feel or sense thoughts and put them into words and feelings. This is the psychic connection. The Psychic-Medium controls the information that they allow themselves to receive therefore respecting and maintaining the privacy of others.

Fear: Attachments! Once you open the door to the non-physical world, there will be entities that will attach themselves to you. That "your light" will attract the demons of hell!

Understanding: The psychic connection is LISTENING to information of the soul memories...it is not an open door to vampires, ghosts, Earth-bound spirits, etc. When we say we are open to the spirit world, it is really just a focus, an intention, to hear what cannot be heard or see what cannot be seen. We intend to work in that world, and only that world.

Fear: "Getting lost" in the psychic realm, to journey and not return to their physical self.

Understanding: When you focus on heightening your psychic senses, you are actually developing a closer relationship to your self, your High Self...you are at a spirit level. There is no where to get lost in. "Going within" is referenced in many religions and it is the same here.

Fear: Fear of death. Some people believe that being psychic or talking to one would introduce information of death and destruction.

Understanding: While it is true that some may get information regarding end of life, this information is also interpreted through the healthy mind and professionalism of the psychic. In other words, it may not always mean death when death is seen through psychic vision. A true psychic never takes free will from their client.

Some people have prophetic dreams of death of those around them or loved ones, or world situations. This is a phenomenon that some people do possess. Prophetic information or things yet to be often come in the form of dreams and begs the question, "why did I get this information." Again, our psychic senses are always picking up information, from soul to soul or the group consciousness of the planet. When that is heightened, we feel it! If this is something you are not experiencing now, you may not develop this sense if you decide to "open" the door. Those who receive this strong prophetic stuff are few and far between.

Fear: A big fear is "everyone is going to think I'm weird!"

Understanding: So what!

Fear: Being woken up at night with ghosts in the room.

Understanding: First, you are always in control of your universe! You may see/hear/feel the energies but that doesn't mean that you are at risk. Also consider that you may have just woken from a dream and still engaging those feelings, sleep paralysis or whatever. Our brains will create a perception according to what our understanding is. If you feel you have ghosts in the room, when you wake up, your brain will create an image, a feeling, etc. There is also a spiritual understanding that our Spirit self leaves at night, goes in and out of the body, and when returning into the body may wake us up and what we feel is a paralysis or confusion on not being in control of our voice, what we see, to what is going on, to and including images of ghosts, being held down by spirit. The other thing is our intention is to receive information only when we want to...we are not always "open" or "on." We set the rules of our psychic selves.

<u>Fear</u>: Feeling everyone's energy, feelings

<u>Understanding</u>: That is being empathic...not pathetic. You are not a victim here! As stated before, you are always in control and that includes how you react to the energies you are feeling or experiencing. You may be someone that feels they are sensitive to everyone else's emotions and and/or physical ailments, and may tend to judge them as "negative" or "positive". Sometimes they are...sometimes they are not. You may be just experiencing someone's mood. These are energies outside of you and you do not need to own them. Try not to get caught up in drama words and phrases that constrict your experience...such as:

- "I pick up *everyone's* energy, feelings, etc.
- "I can *never* go to a mall or in a room with a lot of people"
- "I *always* feel everyone's negative moods."
- "I feel *everything*!"

To change your perspective, try:

- "I feel a lot of energy from others"
- "I experience a lot in crowded spaces."
- "I am sensitive to the moods of others."

- "I sense emotions and physical sensations from many sources."

When you reframe your reaction, you are stepping away from the negative thought and moving toward self empowerment. Then, your world becomes easier.

<u>Myth</u>: Everywhere you go, you will experience ghosts, or spirits.

<u>Understanding</u>: If that is what you intend, then it will be so. Otherwise, again, you are in control of what you experience. We do not believe it to be beneficial to you or anyone else to be in constant, full open, communication with the energy or Spirit. You set your own boundaries as it benefits your own life. Perhaps you are empathic, see above.

<u>Myth</u>: You are open to Spirit "all the time" and if you tell them to "go away" they will never return.

<u>Understanding</u>: If you are hearing/seeing/sensing Spirit (voices, spirits of others) you are creating boundaries; you are not banishing. You might say to them "from the hours of 10 pm to 6 am, I'm sleeping, don't bother me." You may say make appointment times, or "I will be available from 7 to 7:30 am tomorrow morning. Sit with a journal and keep that appointment. Spirit can be like a petulant child. LOL. You need to tell them what to do and when to do it, respectfully of course. So if you make the decision to open to Spirit, make time for them in your life and do it in a way that works for you. Don't be a martyr. Spirit will never leave you. It is our natural existence and all are connected. We are One.

Myth: Psychic-Mediums can't "read" for themselves.

Understanding: While it is difficult to be unbiased (and not emotionally attached) with regards to information of yourself, it can be done. Trust is the key here, and knowing where you are emotionally and mentally when you asked the question. Sometimes we just don't want to hear the information! Some people may choose to use a divination tool, such as a pendulum or tarot cards, to assist in garnering the information from Spirit for themselves. So it doesn't mean you can't do it...it may mean you need to get past your filters, to listen and understand what is being revealed.

Myth: A medium can't do a reading for a close friend or family member "I know too much."

Understanding: This is another self-limiting belief. As much as you think you know about a person, there are many levels of information that can be tapped to receive from Spirit. Acknowledge what you know about them, and look for deeper levels of information, perspective, etc.

Myth: You have to be born with psychic-medium abilities.

Understanding: Nope. While some people do keep their psychic-medium connection from birth, this isn't prerequisite. There are some people more "naturally attuned" but just like in music, we can all sing a tune, but not everyone sings like Pavarotti. Social stigmas, cultural beliefs, lifestyle, religion, etc., cause us to lose this natural connection but we believe this is an ability, to hone the psychic (non-physical) senses, and interpret what is being received.

Myth: Psychic-mediums should not charge for their services (because it's a gift, not a real service, etc.).

Understanding: *We gotta eat!* Like any other professional service, there will be an exchange of value...usually money...for the services rendered. Remember that professional mediums are running a business, whether in their homes or in an office, there are still rent, business expenses, salaries, etc. You can ask your psychic-medium if they'll take chickens, but most likely they will not.

Myth: Psychic-Mediums are pagan, witches, wizards, etc.

Understanding: Being Psychic-Mediums is a life-style, has nothing to do with a religious belief, however there are religions based solely on mediumship. These religions were formed to protect mediums from religious persecution. They are religions of free-thinking and open-mindedness; i.e., Spiritualism, Wiccan/Pagan.

Many mediums will have Rev. before their name; this is a form of legally protecting themselves.

Myth: Psychic-Mediums get information from Facebook, etc., before your appointment.

Understanding: Nope. The information given in a reading would far outweigh any information that one would find on the internet, such as your deceased grandmother's favorite flavor of ice cream!

Myth: If you're psychic, why don't you win the lottery?

Understanding: If you are meant to win the lottery, you will. Everyone gets intuitive hits on games of chance...because it is our innate nature. A psychic-medium may be able to give you lottery numbers however they may not be pertinent in the days in which you buy the tickets for. It is our experience that because we view time here as linear but in the energy side of things, there is no time...time has no meaning. There is so much more going on with your life, life purpose, that "winning the lottery" is perhaps not in the cards.

Myth: Psychic-Mediums believe in EVERYTHING supernatural, metaphysical or other worldly beings.

Understanding: We each have our own belief system, and understanding of the non-physical which creates our core values on which we base our work. We are all like snowflakes, no two are alike. Our understanding of the universe and our part in it is personally ours. This is a wide open field and because we all have our own experiences, that changes how we look at our universe. Each opinion has value but is not necessarily correct for everyone.

Fear: That you can't give a psychic-medium your "real" name for fear that they would look up your information on Google.

Understanding: The professional psychic-medium has no desire to do so. First of all, there is no time to do any prior investigative work, and second, the information on Google. Just as we say the mediums have filters, so do clients. In this case, the client may need to wait to be in a more open frame of mind.

Our fears and myths created to explain them are a result of thousands of years of a limited world view. Today, in an age of greater consciousness awareness and a universe of pure potential energy, we are in a position to create a new world view to include the connection to a greater reality, powerfully, simply and without fear.

Chapter Seventeen

"Let us train our minds to desire what the situation demands."
--Seneca

Energies, Entities and Epiphanies

You don't have to be a medium to sense other energies or entities around us. Sensing energies is sensing the vibrations of things around you...sensing entities are sensing the nature or essence of a person or being.

You will probably hear or come across many instances of "what was that?" Sensing energies come in all forms: Cosmic (planets/moon), Earth, Physical and Non-Physical. So here is a list of types of energies that you may feel or encounter.

Energies:

"Energy is a property of objects, transferable among them via fundamental interactions, which can be converted in form but not created or destroyed." --Wikipedia

Electromagnetic fields of all frequencies represent one of the most common and fastest growing environmental influences, about which anxiety and speculation are spreading. All populations are now exposed to varying degrees of EMF, and the levels will continue to increase as technology advances.

Geopathic Stress is what the body feels due to earth currents from the electromagnetic forces on the earth.

Barometric Pressure Changes – causes pain and inflammation in the body of many people in the form of joint pain, sinus headaches and migraines.

Moon Phases and Planetary Effects – From Mercury in Retrograde to predicting birth of babies by the full moons, humanity has been influenced by the positions of the planets and the moon. It has been documented that gravity and magnetic forces affect the human nervous system, circulatory, hormones, and brain wave activity when unusual cosmic events occur.

People Energies – "Mob Mentality" – A collection of emotionally charged people that can be sensed and is taken on and expanded. Individual energies can also be sensed, person to person.

Elementals – These are life force energies that are of the nature kingdom and are associated with flowers, plants, water, and air. These are commonly referred to as elf, fairy, water sprites, air nymphs, and fire salamanders. Everyday experiences such as taking care of plants, hugging a tree, walking in nature, standing by the ocean, etc., are examples of how you might feel these energies.

Entities

"An *entity* is something that exists in itself, actually or hypothetically. It need not be of material existence." --Wikipedia

Ghosts – A ghost is a spirit that manifests itself so that people can see or hear them. Most often ghosts are thought to be attached to a specific place (home, business, land). There is a belief that when people see ghosts that they are an earth-bound spirit. Our belief is that if a Spirit shows themselves, they want to be seen. They are not stuck anywhere, here or there. If we have free will and choice, then so do they.

Intelligent Spirit – In terms of paranormal work, an intelligent spirit is one who engages ghost busters through electronic equipment; for example, voice recordings, electromagnetic field meters, infrared thermometers, etc. A medium would call an "intelligent spirit" just a spirit!

Residual Energy – This is thought to be an energetic recording of an event that imprints itself on a specific place. For example, in Gettysburg, PA, people would hear canon fire in the evening coming from the battlefield. These are energetic memories, not the ghosts of the soldiers re-enacting the battle.

Poltergeist Activity – This is a spirit that can manifest enough energy to move objects.

Visitations and Dreams – Most visitations will happen just after passing. There are many people who say they have seen their loved ones who have shown themselves and they find out later that it was at their moment of passing. People also have visitations in dream states. The brain slows down and all the chatter of day is not there...this is the natural channel at its purest. This is the easiest way to receive because there are no barriers, no critical thinking. We are open to dreams. A visitation dream is clear and memorable. You would swear they were there...and they were!

Susan: My great aunt Verona had passed who was my grandmother's sister. She wore her hair red and had it done just so. Verona was a reserved woman, kind and quiet. One month after she passed, I was with my aunt and grandmother and said "I dreamt about Aunt Verona last Thursday night." My aunt and my grandmother took hold of each other's hands. They looked spooked and said "tell us about your dream." I told them that I had seen Aunt Verona sitting at the end of a very long table. I couldn't see any other faces, but was very aware and surprised to see Aunt Verona laughing heartily and throwing her head back as she laughed. This was very out of character for her. The two women looked at each other and asked me, "What was she wearing?" but we all answered together, "a turquoise dress." As it turned out, the three of us had the same dream, on the same night. We all were left feeling Verona was happy and relaxed.

Epiphanies

An epiphany is "a manifestation of a divine or supernatural being."

We may also see spirit without knowing we see spirit...they are right there in front of us and we believe they are a living person.

Susan had a dear friend while growing up whose home she spent a lot of time in, and so she knew her parents quite well. Her father was a striking man, tall. He stood like a military man, erect posture. He had thick wavy hair, thick eyebrows and big green eyes...a very handsome man. About 25-30 years later, Susan was driving down the street and in front of the house they lived in, she saw Mr. Henry. He was walking on the sidewalk in front of the home. She recognized him from his posture and as she drove by, looked right at his face and recognized him. She thought, "Wow, he is now gray and still such a handsome man." and drove on. Three weeks later, Susan was introduced to her brothers' new girlfriend introduced to me as Jan. After some conversation, I asked her where she grew ~~and~~ up and she told me the name of the street. So I asked her last name and it was "Henry." Are you Cindy's sister? And she said "Yes!" So I told her I had known her parents as a young person and that I had just seen her father in front of the house and how great he looked. She looked at me, with eyes wide open and said "thank you...I was wondering if he was ok." He had passed away three years earlier. Susan had seen him as plain as day along the street, and would not have known she had seen spirit if it were not for the conversation.

We also hear stories of historical places where guests will ask about the people they saw in the specific areas. The curator or docent would respond that there were no such people in that area. There are also stories where people know they have had an experience with someone, an interesting conversation or event that was also very helpful to them....and come to find out it was considered an angel visit.

People also connect with the loved ones who have passed directly...meaning, they did not go see a medium, but had experiences that they knew it was their mom, dad, sister, etc. They would feel them sit on the side of their bed, or smell their favorite perfume or cigar, and see something in nature that would just instantly remind them.

From the cosmos, to the earth's pulse, to the body's senses, and memories of those who have passed, these are all examples of our natural connection to the energy around us.

CHAPTER EIGHTEEN

Kids say *and see* the darndest things...

Children will experience seeing, and sensing, Spirit because they have not developed the filters the adult has that block this information. They have not yet had the life experiences, the social stigmas, the cultural beliefs or fears that create these blocks. Their innocence, their trust, is wide open. If a child sees their deceased grandma in their bedroom, they trust it's grandma!

When a child says they see a person, like the imaginary friend, more often than not, this child is seeing Spirit, energy, or a part of themselves they need at the time, either emotionally, developmentally, etc. When the child relays these experiences to their parents, and the parents react negatively to it through their fears or beliefs, the child then picks up that filter, eventually blocking further interaction with Spirit or energy.

If a child is upset that they are seeing the spirit of a deceased loved one, you can relate this to their imagination by asking them to close their eyes and see that person in their head. Tell the child that sometimes the mind can see what the imagination is telling them. Their imagination is so strong that their eyes will see it and the child will not be able to tell the difference. Imagination is engaged when connecting to the non-physical world, so the parent is not negating the fact the child is actually seeing spirit but allows the parent to explain the sixth sense. This then is done in a way that the child understands that what they are seeing is not bad, and hopefully alleviates the fear of seeing a dead person.

There are many times the incidents of sensing energies don't fully go away, and the child is left dealing with a part of themselves they now feel is wrong or in danger. Instead of the parent telling the child that what they see is not there, it can be very empowering to allow the child to fully explain what they see and feel, and not to react fearfully or negatively. This allows the child to trust the parent with this kind of experience in the future.

Children will have dreams or even nightmares to relieve some of the stress of not understanding, or having the ability to express, these experiences. Dreams can also be attributed to spirit communication or as a result of unsettled energy (and emotions) inside the home. A good way to deal with a child who is having these stressful times is to have them draw what they are seeing or feeling. This gives the child a way to release as well as provide a sense of trust between child and parent. And as stated earlier, trust is key when developing this communication channel.

Kinetic energy is telekinesis and the ability to move objects with the mind. Children and teens are most likely to do this involuntarily reaction from mental or emotional stresses, hormonal changes, and discord in the family/home. People believe when they have objects moving in their home that they have a ghost or poltergeist, when in fact a child is responsible for moving the objects with kinetic energy. Before calling in the ghost-busters, a family can review the stress situation in the home, talk with the kids, and begin to intentionally ease the anxieties. A medium can go into the home, feel and sense the energies and discuss with the family the sources of the activity.

Indigo and Crystal Children

There are an increasing number of labels being put on children who are more aware of their environment and energies today, and range from Indigo, Crystal, Rainbow, Star, etc. Children today are more learned about their selves, sensitive to the energies around them, and have the freedom to express and experience psychic phenomena. However, they are not special children...they are our children living in an age of information and open minds.

Connie: While at a psychic fair, a woman and her teen daughter came to our table and wanted to ask a question. The question was "I was told my daughter is a Crystal Child...do you know anything about that?" I explained what I knew about the theory of Indigo and Crystal children, in that the generations born in the 20th and 21st centuries are more aware of their natural connection to the unseen world, and that their psychic senses were not hushed or discouraged as before. I also discussed that these were labels of not special children but of a fantastic time in our history where our natural intuitions and connections to Spirit are encouraged, to not feel like a freak, and to embrace them. I felt that the explanation would help to alleviate the fears of the mother, and the anxieties of the daughter. However, the mother looked dismayed and walked away. We then assumed she may have wanted more fanfare around her daughter's "special" gifts than provided, which only will alienate her daughter more from her peers.

When do you know your child is sensitive to energies that you do not see?

- The imaginary friend.
- Having a full blown conversation when no one else is around.
- When the child gives you information regarding a loved one passed that they never knew or met.
- When children see colors or shimmering lines around things or people, which are auras.
- An uncanny sense to know what someone is going to do or say next.
- The child is seeing shadows and may feel fearful or threatened.
- Children also draw pictures of their family only they add extra people floating above.
- The child reports that they are seeing a person they know who is deceased.
- When the child sees a scary or unknown figure in their room, and repeats the same description over and over.

Today, there are many resources to aid parents with a sensitive child. Not only through the internet, but through professional mediums who have an understanding of these energies, can relate to their experiences, relieve their fears and let them know it is a natural channel to access.

Chapter Nineteen

"I think we are here for each other."
–Carol Burnett

Where do you find a Psychic-Medium?

Everywhere! Just look in the mirror!

There are several types of venues you may see a psychic-medium work. Probably the most common venue is at a psychic fair, where many psychic-mediums will set up their reading areas and conduct one-on-one readings to the general public. This is a great place to see a variety of reading types, such as tarot, crystal ball, medium, palm, astrology, etc., as well as get a glimpse of the medium before signing up for a reading. A lot of people get a feeling for a particular medium and go with that.

There are mediums who have set up private practices at their home or at a local business (most often but not limited to metaphysical stores) for private readings, including seeing a psychic reading taking place in a local coffee shop.

There are Spiritualist Churches, spiritual organizations and communities where mediums who regularly serve to provide messages are a part of the service.

Psychic-Mediums may also offer group readings, where readings are offered to a group of people at a time. Depending on the number of people and the time allotted, this may be a shorter reading directed at one person at a time, or "opening to Spirit" and going to any of the people in the group when appropriate.

Gallery-style or demonstration style reading events are when the mediums are at the front of a larger group of people, offering information about mediumship, their experiences, Q&A as well as brief messages to a sampling of the audience.

Many psychic-mediums today are called to do group or private readings parties at home, special family events such as birthdays, reunions, etc., or even corporate events.

Websites offer listings of mediums in your area, as well as website of the medium to offer on-line readings. One of the best ways to get a good medium is to ask...referrals are still a powerful source.

There are no limits to the ways a psychic-medium can offer their insights and services to their community.

Conclusion
The Daily Medium

"You unlock this door with the key of imagination. Beyond it is another dimension - a dimension of sound, a dimension of sight, a dimension of mind. You're moving into a land of both shadow and substance, of things and ideas. You've just crossed over into the Twilight Zone."

Well, this may sound scarier than it is when presented as *The Twilight Zone*, but offers the other view of the world from the perspective of the psychic-medium.

The only "dimension" we refer to is the non-physical as a change in mindset and belief, away from fear and superstition, to accept the input and interpretation of these unseen energies and make sense of them in an everyday reality.

Through our right and left brains, through our physical and non-physical senses, we can explore and engage the energies in this natural channel of communication. This natural channel makes us all, in essence, psychic-mediums. It is inherent in our being, our DNA, our existence here on Earth and it can be incorporated into our daily lives.

Throughout this book, we've talked about the normalness of psychic-medium communication, by understanding our selves, our connection with a Higher Power, and the energies in the universe around us. We understand our selves through balance of beliefs and awareness, that we are not only a part of something greater than ourselves, we are One with that something! A "spiritual being having a human experience" in a universe that behaves consistently and simplistically, without judgment or mythology.

The Daily Medium is a Facebook page of inspirational sayings and experiences:

> *The Daily Medium knows to not only define who we are, but divine who we are. God, Creator, I Am, Infinite Intelligence, Universe, Mother, Father...doesn't matter what you name your higher power, doesn't matter what you call it. All that matters is that you call it! That you understand that there is something that keeps us going other than blood and organs. The Daily Medium is at work with this higher power every day, all day. The Daily Medium knows that this higher power is expressed through all of us and everything around us. All we need to do is listen and feel what our heart is saying. Take a moment today to acknowledge your sense of the love that is being hurled your way! Breathe it in and move forward in your day. Enjoy!*

Thank you for joining us!

Appendix

Resources

Ask and It Is Given by Esther and Jerry Hicks

Conversations with God by Neale Donald Walsch

Infinite Possibilities – The Art of Living Your Dreams by Mike Dooley (tut.com)

Infinite Quest by John Edward

Self Matters by Phillip C. McGraw, PhD

Super Soul Sunday – oprah.com

The Four Agreements by Don Miguel Ruiz

The Power of Intention by Wayne Dyer

The Secret by Rhonda Byrne

The Seven Spiritual Laws of Success by Deepak Chopra, MD

The White Eagle Lodge – whiteeaglelodge.org

We are All Born Mediums by Paul and Deborah Rees

What the Bleep do We Know – whatthebleep.com

GLOSSARY

Clear (as in clearing a space) – To purposefully dissipate dull, old or negative energies left over by a person or event.

Chakras – Energy centers that interact through the nervous and endocrine systems of the body.

Energies – The basic vibes of the universe, Life Force, etc.

Entities – When energies take and behave in "human form" or when we perceive energies in human form or characteristic.

High Self – The "spark" of the Divine, full consciousness of its divinity and purpose, also referred to as the Authentic Self.

Medium – Receiving information from those who have passed

Mind – Body – Spirit – The elements of expressing life through awareness of our mental, emotional, physical and spiritual bodies.

Other Side – Meant to convey "the other side" of life, it refers to the non-physical world, of energy and spirit. Also referred to as Heaven

Psychic – Receiving information from living things

Realm – Just another word for world.

Sacred space – a dedicated area to connect within, to journal, pray, meditate, etc.

Sitter – This is the client, the one the medium is doing the reading for.

Spirit (capital S) – This is the reference to the Cosmic Consciousness and the Divine Realm of Its location

spirit (small s) – the spirit of the self

Soul – The aspect of the High Self that holds all the experiences, wisdom and memories of its existences.

Source – Another name for God, God Consciousness, Infinite Intelligence, etc.

Subtle Bodies – Physical, Mental, Emotional, Spiritual – The aspects of the energies associated with expression of the High Self

Tune in – Connecting to the energies and the loved ones who have passed. Also known as making a link.

Vibrations – The frequency of energies

Made in the USA
Columbia, SC
18 October 2022